Padam Padam

KEVIN KILLIAN

Padam Padam

COLLECTED POEMS

EDITED BY
EVAN KENNEDY
AND JASON MORRIS

INTRODUCTION BY
KAY GABRIEL

Nightboat Books
New York

Cover image of Kevin Killian in 1989. Photo by Loring McAlpin.

Printed in the United States

ISBN: 978-1-643-62290-3

Design and typesetting by Kit Schluter
Typeset in Plantin MT Pro and **ACUMIN VARIABLE CONCEPT**

Cataloging-in-publication data is available
from the Library of Congress

Nightboat Books
New York
www.nightboat.org

Contents

Introduction

Here's a story from Kevin Killian's memoir *Bedrooms Have Windows*, in a chapter titled "Poetry." He goes to a reading in New York by the poet Ted Berrigan and discovers he doesn't understand Berrigan's writing at all. In response to what feels like humiliation, Killian steals first the hors d'oeuvres, then the wine, then "hundreds of pills—probably Ted's also . . . it was like *Valley of the Dolls*." Then the youthful Kevin Killian hits the road and travels, cowboy style, west to California, leaving New York behind for good.

I'd be surprised if anything like that really happened. It feels instead like one of Kathy Acker's fables about real, famous people, but with more allegory to it. (Some evidence: Killian says elsewhere[1] that Berrigan, Ginsberg and Plath were his favorite poets before he moved to California and got involved in the New Narrative movement—more on that shift in taste below.) Decode the allegory: Killian steals outrageously from another to produce a totally different creative result. It's never actually derivative, except in the most literal possible terms. Killian takes a title or a proper name or lyrics and puts all that to work in new and alien ways. In prose, in poets theater, and in his poetry, Killian practices Bertolt Brecht's principle that repurposing familiar language, image, and encounter makes new consciousness possible. Is that grandiose?—have I gone too far for a body of work that collages B movies, advertising copy, and the lyrics of Kylie Minogue, that explicitly downplays its own seriousness? Forgive me, Kevin, I think it's the truth.

1. In the introduction to *Writers Who Love Too Much: New Narrative Writing, 1977-1997*, eds. Killian and Dodie Bellamy (Nightboat: 2017), xv.

In contrast to his fiction (*Spreadeagle, Shy*, the stories collected in *Impossible Princess*) and memoir (*Fascination*), Killian's poetry more rigorously and thoroughly places a third term between itself and its object. To write *Argento Series*, his first book, Killian followed a suggestion from Acker to write about the catastrophe of the AIDS crisis in San Francisco through the horror films of Dario Argento. His second, *Action Kylie*, puts Kylie Minogue to work. Killian, both addressing and in drag as Kylie, borrows an insight from camp sensibility that total adoration makes its object more interesting and capacious. Similar principles of composition apply, in whole or in part, for the other books and chapbooks collected in this volume: *Tweaky Village, Tony Greene Era, Elements*.

Throughout these exercises in riff and quotation, Killian is almost always in drag: as Kylie Minogue as the Green Fairy in Baz Luhrmann's *Moulin Rouge*, as a tweaker who "lost ME to METH," as Frank O'Hara acting perfectly disgraceful, as Tim Dlugos intoning that "the corpses change but the party goes on forever." The drag changes, sometimes, from poem to poem, or line to line—like, Kevin, you did it again! In the spirit of literary drag, Killian never means "I" straightforwardly when he says it, not even when the "I" really *really* is Kevin Killian. Playing these "city games"—a section title in *Action Kylie* that he pinched from a rumored but never released Kylie Minogue album—makes it possible for a reader, in her own drag as Kevin Killian, to encounter old problems, curiosities and terrors from new and productively strange perspectives. Think of it as an experiment in collective language, in which mouthing someone else's words in a different context transforms the speech no less than the speaker.

Check out, for instance, Killian's poem "Good Like That," which reworks the lyrics from the title track off of Kylie Minogue's *Fever*, and threads them together with an extended draggy riff on the minor scandal from the early 2000s where Jeb Bush's daughter attempted to forge a prescription for downers:

> My little nephew in the Persian Gulf says
> His heart is beating faster and
> War is a disaster
> Slick in a white uniform, his head shaved, the top of his head a white ball

Oh! Noelle Bush, work is a disaster, I needed that Xanax
just to get me through the day of new job for internet
start-up, I called my own number saying, I am doctor Kevin Killian . . .

And driving to prescription
My mom will have conniptions
I'm good like that
I can speak for US Navy, and my boys will come and save me
Sans souci, but I need to get my mouth round that Xanax
it helps me with my panics
It's good like that
The news is like a hairline
receding on the airline . . .

Hi, it's me—Noelle Bush, and that is my pre-
scription I called in on the phone machine with my
number of love from doctor Kevin what the fuck
is his name now???

Notice how Kylie's unbeatable hook, "Heart is beating faster and work is a disaster," provides a rhythmic, rhyming pattern for Killian to riff on, in progressively more jangly and almost compulsive tones, "navy-save me," "xanax-panics," "hairline-airline." Killian's collage breathes life into a whole universe of feeling: a forcefully cheery mania maintained mid-war. Does that sound familiar? As for the melodrama of Noelle Bush and Doctor Kevin Killian, the poem's slapstick feels less like an MSNBC-style laugh at hypocritical Republicans xanning out and more like Kevin Killian acting the actual disaster of work on the stage of celebritized desperation: even the political class feels this thing, the need to get numb "just to get me through the day of new job," and of course they do, because they can't escape the world they made either, as fatal as it's also breathlessly humiliating.

Killian uses his detournement to think in thickly structured and surprisingly open ways about loss, disaster, glamor, sex, cities, genre, gay life, war, gentrification, premature death. He typically does it humorously, and makes his attack in a wry but never ironic spirit. His comic instinct lets him jump into and out of clowning, playing the Fool to us distracted, prideful Lears. But it's not all jokes, and his verse is rarely light. Killian frequently wrote elegy, and his grief is more moving for its substantial humor. And although he deprecated his own talent as "second or third rate," Killian was also a frankly *virtuosic* lyric poet with a singular ear for beautiful, disturbing language. "Secret lives in a post-gay economy, / where I could marry you—or you—tomorrow, / and in the space of an hour could lose my female hormones / to a non-matriculating major of Penn," come *on*!

What's the cumulative effect of all this wild combination, what does it look like in practice, how did Killian even get there? While he bypassed the dead weight of gravitas that a lot of US poetry adopts by default, Killian also took poetry seriously enough for it to have the function of religion—in the sense of assembling a community dedicated to determining meaning in round after round of structured play and deliberate interpretation. Killian drew this lesson from, among other sources, the San Francisco poet Jack Spicer (1925-65), whose biography he co-authored with Lew Ellingham, and whose collected poems he co-edited with Peter Gizzi. A basically neglected poet when Killian and his collaborators worked on their books about him, Spicer combined his militant anti-professionalism with a profound faith in poetry as a vocation understood and experienced through dedicated, repeated, communal practice.

Spicer's emphasis on the community that makes poetry function found a welcome audience in the Bay Area's New Narrative movement, which Killian enthusiastically participated in nearly from its start, and whose writers collectively and individually emphasize the role of the social in artistic production. Killian and Dodie Bellamy in their introduction to *Writers Who Love Too Much*, their anthology of New Narrative, specifically compare New Narrative's "writing prompted . . . by community" to Spicer's "Poetry and Magic" workshop, "when [Spicer] was writing books in which every poem was written for a different person he knew." Only where the coteries of the San Francisco Renaissance sometimes tended small and insular, Killian, bolstered by New Narrative's pro-social ethos, magnanimously expanded the poetic community that he stewarded—through Poets Theater performances, reading series invitations, personal correspondence, editing others' manuscripts. One could get drunk on his admiration, his warmth and support. With a thoroughly genuine attention and a mighty mental Rolodex, Killian made the people around him feel like the stars of stage and screen whose autographs he collected, as if he was your fan, and not the other way around. His tactfulness and generosity of spirit set an example: Killian treated poetry as a social infrastructure through which people can come to recognize each other as part of a shared project.

Through Spicer, Killian also adopted and showed generation after generation of other poets the force of the serial poem, in which the meaning of a project becomes clear through the scale and repetition of a series rather than through isolated poetic encounters. "There really is no single poem," Spicer wrote in his book *Admonitions*. "Poems should echo and re-echo against each other. They should create resonances. They cannot live alone any more than we can." Spicer's serial poetics makes it possible to write, and to write ambitiously, without producing individually perfect poems, or even poems that are good verse all the way through. You can breathe a little easier, because the series does the work that no poem, however finely polished, could accomplish.

Killian's *Argento Series* made a principle out of this formal mechanism, which he repeated through the years: in the Kylie poems in and after *Action Kylie*, in *Elements*, in his "Soft Art" poems. Similar to the abundance of drag personae Killian adopts, his irrepressible seriality activates his work's ambition. Killian's seriality scales up poetry's capacity to confront, distort, sully, transform. Consider *Argento Series* again: Killian exits the limbo of individuated pain, building an overarching perspective on avoidable catastrophe through each poem's trenchant, particular mourning.

There's a lesson here for people who want poetry to be a form of structured thought with social and even political force. How does anybody use poetry to talk about real situations that matter to people in a way that makes a lick of difference for them, and doesn't just recite already known facts in fancier than normal language? Killian isn't a political poet *per se*, but his abundant body of work offers real answers to these more than aesthetic problems. He turns his games of language and persona into big, usable architectures for understanding social crises, or making militantly absurd fun of routinized humiliation, or figuring out how anyone experiences reality in a society in which profit terrorizes people and commodities take on lives of their own "and nobody knows their business, not even the moguls at Skywalker Ranch who control everything else." Try his poem "Jealous Roommate" for a really short, punchy *ars poetica*:

> "And why do you write?" she said to me.
> She's everyone from A to Z.
> "I write," I said, "because it's fun,
> Because, like Jell-O,
> I have been invented."

I have a postcard of this poem somewhere. On it, Killian has illustrated his own words in bright colored pencil, as if to underscore the points in his defense.

Am I calling Killian a secret *formalist*? Sort of. He's insouciant towards received forms—witness his broken sestina "Get Outta My Way"—but makes routine practice out of wordplay, punning, riffing, anagrams, palindromes, acrostics and other patterns of strategically prioritizing form over content. Killian's play yields deliriously apt results. "No real charm beneath Helena Bonham Carter," he writes in his anagrams. In his palindromes: "Eva, can I stab bats in a cave? // No, Mel Gibson is a casino's big lemon." Language, in Killian's hands, reveals surprise truths, as if he conducted a seance, or sat in the analyst's chair. In that sense, his playfulness, like his humor, always has an oblique purpose. You might follow its slips to the truth you know but could not see, or to the something important that he saw but couldn't remember.

But I don't mean to accuse Killian of all this weighty stuff, like revealing truth and transforming reality, without also crediting him for authoring a fabulous, permissive body of work, charming, filthy and smarmy at turns, with its retchable milk enemas and its devilish twists on Hölderlin's "Pallaksch." It's as if he's always stopping to say hey to some bright gem of cultural refuse, and figuring out how he can set it into his language palace. Thank God we get to live there forever, too. Like Brecht and Kurt Weill said about their *Rise and Fall of the City of Mahagonny*, Kevin Killian is fun. He's more fun than you or I can bear, and we have to, have to, keep bearing his wit.

I don't need anyone to copy Kevin Killian's accomplishments, or adopt his dreams as their own, any more than one might attempt to recreate Kylie Minogue's 1997 trip hop album *Impossible Princess* from scratch. Instead, look at what Killian made possible through his practice, his own particular discipline, his dedication to others, his voracious cultural and intellectual appetites. The stakes are so high, actually, for a queer culture that's both *fun*, as in *actually desirable to live in*, and capable of thinking through crisis. Thank God—and thank Dodie Bellamy, Evan Kennedy, Jason Morris, and Nightboat Books—that his collected poems are now in print. The poems you're about to read aren't just some kind of bliss. They're a master class in mediation. They're queasy. They're writhing off the page. And metabolized in your mouths and thoughts they're about to live another life, and another.

—KAY GABRIEL

Editors' Note

We made a good duo for several reasons. Both of us were Kevin's friends and attentive readers while he was here, and we found, in returning to his poems, even more reason to read closely and respond. After Kevin's wife, Dodie Bellamy, sent us Kevin's hard drive, we separately compared the five books of poetry with the manuscripts, then met and made all obvious corrections.

Evan was perhaps better at fact-checking, catching the odd misspelled name; Jason maybe with questions of formatting. Our real obligation to Kevin, and to his poems, was never lost on us—we approached this undertaking with the reverence which it is due.

Nevertheless, we didn't want to waste any time in getting it to you. So we worked with deliberate speed, which lent us the relative looseness needed to retain amusement and astonishment at these brilliant, freaky, strange, and gorgeous poems. "MILF"—all caps, right? This line should break between "got" and "fucked." Correct spelling of *skeezy*, or Kevin's? Just wondering: where did Kevin get the line "Cause my body too bootylicious for ya, baby"? There were myriad song, film, and art titles Kevin hipped us to (again!).

Do we capitalize the "v" and "d" of Valentine's Day? Or leave it lower case, with no apostrophe, as he has it? We tended to pick the "abject" over the "correct." As "Nude Valentine" reminds us, slang is the language love learns first.

On a structural level, we decided to move Kevin's first four "Elements" poems, originally published in *Tony Greene Era* and later republished as part of a longer series in *The Elements*, to the *Elements* section of this book. We also decided to add seven previously unpublished "Elements"; these are the last poems in the present collection.

During this project, Kylie Minogue's "Padam Padam" became a summer anthem. We heard it thumping from cars and clubs all over San Francisco. It was bittersweet; Kevin was her biggest fan. We associate quite a few places here with Kevin, like the bookstore where he'd host readings or the Subway where he'd lunch with poets. Now he was there wherever we heard the song—Pride weekend in Dolores Park, or at a bar in SoMa. Kevin wouldn't have called "Padam Padam" a comeback, though everyone dancing that foggy summer treated it like one.

While out clubbing, Kylie locks eyes with someone familiar. A shiver jolts her. Hearts flutter, a prelude to an unforgettable encounter: *padam padam*. Like a bright pop-cultural heartbeat across the darkening decades, Kevin's poems—always much more than a one-night stand—will trace his love of fantasy, his humor, and his larger-than-life generosity for a new audience.

—EVAN KENNEDY AND JASON MORRIS

ARGENTO SERIES

for

KATHY ACKER
DODIE BELLAMY
SCOTT HEIM
STEVEN SHAVIRO
GARY SMITHSON AND
JULIANA SPAHR

through whom in the first place
I read the work of Dario Argento

"I saw something important I can't remember"

Stage Fright

The Bird with the Crystal Plumage

Hey, *goombah*, c'mere,
I've built a flotilla of words to this
    vein in your arm!

Hola, guy, who used to
IV a grow horn in my
    vitals, come on, *andale,*

Here's the big bird
I've built out of crystal
    very cool and white and wet, a swan

high above San Francisco
in a clear winter—
    vite, vite!

Hop on my back
I'll take you there to
    volunteer for the Shanti Project

Happy trails
In the skyways American
    valedictory flock, geese

Help me, I think
I'm falling in looooooooooooooo-
    -ve with you

Giallo

Cut to theme music: brass, strings, zither, giallo
the word bursts in red spectacular fire, soon
muted to a dull yellow like mustard

It's the angle, it's the hook they keep telling
me in the front office, in New York, demons eat them
Wal, blow me down with one of those new fangled

Ok, thought of something bound to beat the
bandolero: mod two in white—battle—killer in the
rain, and the white, wet, reveals shadowy skin

looking like sexuality
talk to Mr. Gabriel
get those asses into those seats

then he gives her a blowjob
the camera pulls back, way, back, sky high
it's a football field of dead men in trenches

doesn't look so scary
it's not like Juliette Lewis
no, it's musical, with glockenspiel
telling the people, *go home now, I love you,*
your breath makes me love you,
in AIDS is pleasure

Steve Abbott told me, when we go we
go into a blank space, like an envelope,
on our way to who? Are you Kevin? he asked me.
The bed a big waste basket of white cotton.

Tracking Shot

The job unfinished. The killer's POV. Long hair blowing in the wind
(nameless) an excellent target for bazookas. Thunderous goblin music.

At the moment between now and falling asleep the ghosts rush in. I'm
45, time for ghosts, the dead fluttering their scarves

like Isadora. Duncan. Snap. Head popped off, sails across the screen
like popcorn fresh in the big glass warm box, boy's nose pressed against
it watching

to the thunderous goblin music. Grabs the boy, curiously not kicking,
perhaps a bundle of rags, and drags him up the side of the house

across the roof, avoiding the mansards

down the other side of the house. Through the east windows the
beautiful woman is writing her name on a misted porcelain surface
with her last breath

I blow on it, the text disappears, the name of the killer.
Up over the house. "I'll call him my 'HOUSE BOY,'" the killer laughs,
to thunderous goblin music. Maybe it sounds more realistic in Italian.
I hate it when they can't afford real babies or boys

and have to use dummies made of rags, you always know
that's not a baby

the cold air fills the hot wet room like an eraser blanket, now I can't
read the killer's name. All she can write is H

and looked at it another way it is I

and upside down, kicking, V

I am reading these signs of the infidel hates me

Deep Red

Deep red • the submarine blips on the cold surface
in Antarctica • as Mariner's ship draws near •
frothy surface on the blue wave •
Life is still • so catch as catch can • still evanescent, still

Red, an oar touches the water's rim • muscular arm buff as
Meryl Streep's in *The River Wild* • in Antarctica •
frothy surface on the blue wave • life is still • "I don't have
many T cells left, but I used to have 8" • "now I have 9"

Under the gristle, vein, under the vein, deep red •
the blood of my pal • deeper and deeper this tiny wave, blue
on the surface • alone on the surface •
if you were one-dimensional what would you see?
a one celled mammal swimming for dear life •
to a shore strewn with protozoa bracken • still life
"now I have six"

the flotsam and • jetsam of living • high
and deep • this is the curve that
will kill you • pal
I'm living in • your disgrace
deep • red hatchet • cells
a doll with hands • scuttles across the face •
of the sea for you
come and get these • memories

Profondo Thrilling

Now the things that are coming to an end,
who will believe them?
Preposterous mettle, cheeky pets,
he hid them all in the date palm,
while I searched the landscape
the moving portrait
which bled real tears into gullible goblet

When I was twenty-one he was always
there a step older then my soldier
on the streets of Greenwich Village in
jelly shoes, tiger lilies, questions
for Laura
The voice in the suitcase
a man darker and older than

the rainbow, in puddle of oil, Bleecker Street
gutter. You know how you're reading a book,
it's good, the pages on the right
grow thinner,
you don't want it to end, there's a clue
right there in the patchwork quilt,
baby let's swing

Long, red, ropy kind of stiff statuary
Where is the night lustre?
Past my sorrows,
rafting down on the glory river
where I searched for his trail,
the living ball
that glowed an unearthly silvery prick—

Stomach, colon, brain acting up, and
over in Berkeley a magic school
I met him on a Sunday
and he taught me how to skip

week days, smoking his weed, whack,
seven strange clues
to guide me to a future sickness, a child

Least he had the grace to look ashamed
his whole broken-ass mule train
Foolish burro of the north lands,
why do you shy away at strangers?
What's the worst that could happen?
The haunted attic
over your headdress files you under—

I feel it in the ocean, often, the unthinking wave,
Surf white and brown in caps, like
mushrooms that come alive then plink
Red-yellow honey, sassafras and
. . . then it's winter,
black mouth moves in the talking snowman
"Ah, Kevin, you're so jejune"

Brrrr! Talk about frosty! I met him on
the breadline, giving him enormous
kicks in the ass
I never wanted to go, but noting
the strange likeness, moved toward him
like two bananas from the same
clump in bodega

hot summer patchouli night stand
with silver bangles cooling Spanish Harlem
fourth floor porch
ghost parade, shadows vanish
so there I am, egg on my face and
unbelievable growing rock, slowly
erect at a dance I hide with my coat flap

—profondo thrilling— Now the
things that are coming to an end
there is nothing beyond them

but surrey
Wait, buddy boy! Invisible chimes
hang from the theater ceiling, safety curtain
let it come down, thud, swish,

plop. Execution completed,
on the bare stage a man lies dead, his
body a motley of harlequin lights
and black diamonds.
Hide your heart, the yellow phantom
whispers at the corner of the curtain
Places please

Integral Hard

Down in the south land, where every dick
with a woody thinks he's a stickman

along the white pines, Manolo,
we hauled the white pine of Manolo.

Along the white way a man is dead
in the sorry summer of San Tanquera

Manolo, where did he fall
the operation you paid for, with Blue Cross,

your white pine to coffin-size whittled,
Manolo, as though you were a scion of ABBA?

Should the summer heat melt your ice to sweat
sweet as the yellow pine of Manolo Station,

thc suppurated halfway of hair pie
where white, once mentioned, Manolo,

peels from the very bottom of the pile-up traffic
in San Tanquera's loco. I stop and cup my ear:

"White pine! Yellow pine!" howl the dogs
of San Tanquera assaulting Manolo

from either side of the one street in hot town
with one pie, and only two dogs with any hair

as Lee, Senior, falls to the floor
I remember ringing your bell and startled

by the way I'd seen Charles before, on TV,
from Mexican westerns, *Star Trek* re-runs

and frail as you were, Matias and I staring
into one mirrored wall, our society gaze

bouncing to and fro ever diminishing
and poetry, a solid stone on the pine deal table

becoming as the night wore on with much wine
ever so much more solid, the thing itself

outside the hacienda a hairless dog long as
dick itself, Manolo, howled to Mars a la

Charles Bukowski and Leland Hickman and
Orson Welles and every big dream of the world lost

to AIDS and its depredations
the Magnificent seven of your wranglers

lonely father on Calle, quiet pierced by gunshot

for inscrutable bush of mesquite, ablaze,

to depredation encircling AIDS like corrida,
"slovenly wilderness,"
until only red molten ring of the poem itself

lies on your doorstep where once I cooled my heels
thinking
"I'm on the doorstep of fucking *Leland Hickman.*"

Trauma

I didn't want to have the little boy
but I kept him, tuggled, inside my bush.

You don't eat enough, so you're
spilling your chowder like barley.

Pull over here, I got to hurl my trauma
over the rushing water style bridge bridge,

and watch the series of tiny tugboats
take my baby away the lonesome river.

Trauma of losing a pal to AIDS, or SIDA
as he used to tell me while dreaming.

He was in Barcelona watching the Olympics
like Frank O'Hara in love with Bill Berkson.

Phenomena

Don't make me over, I don't want to lose this strange power of mine
I talk to insects
Arranging trains of locusts and spiders

I take AZT, what's with my complexion, or am I shorter
am I losing
my power of command over the insects

What's worse, this rotten medication that kills you with cramps
or the feeling that
soon the insects will ignore me, I'll be this *dumb fuck*

they can walk all over with six legs and eight legs, I won't
be able to say
a word to them, to alter their course in any conceivable way

I was a pretty girl once in the Basque countryside under
Gernikako Arbola
the tree of the insects, till the dwarf knifed away my powers

psychic surgery, now I'm caught between two stools
power to live
power to talk to the insects and they will obey me on trains

Perché Quelle Strane Gocce di Sangue sul Corpo di Jennifer?

December 15, Dodie, scornful, "Is he your
        new boyfriend?" I'm humming and hawing, well
what do you mean, I'm not doing him
        "but would you like to?"

January 3rd or 4th, I'm so sure, 1998 and a
        black night in San Francisco
Why did Peter tell Steve and Jennifer I lived
        miles from the Museum, is he trying to
Destroy me? What are those strange drops
        of blood on the body of Jennifer?
What is that bird big as a duck that's not a
        duck on the grass with a black
Bib and dark tan Stripes, is it a kind of dove
        or pigeon? What would I gain
By knowing? Someone seems to have poured
        mineral oil on my new leather date
Book, my "Time Master" trademark, am
        I coming or going? It's slippery
On the wet surface of our forty steps going
        up, iron piled into flat planes of
Perpendicular, horizontal, all pebbled.

February 25th, Lisa says, "I hear you are
        having rowboat weather, I picture
the cats in bright flotational jackets," was
        "Lisa Says" one of the Velvet Under-
ground songs only a fan like I would treasure
        way back when, those endless
canoodlings on a single theme, a woman
        speaking? "Candy" or "Lisa" or
now I can't remember the third. The
        late sixties or 1971. Anyhow the
rain's not *that* bad. Effective but not dismal.
        Beneath my window it's silver

and watchful, like a woman speaking
in one of Laura Nyro's songs, and
that I can date more precisely. Dodie
would really like to get Marjorie
Perloff to talk about something. Wonder
if the trial has begun, and where?

March 4, Ron Johnson dies at home
(KS).
Waiting
for the other shoe to drop, okay,
clunk. Satisfied? I told him I'd met Peter
(O'Leary), I said, "I love him." His
big eyes shaking under the scars of all
those operations. "*But I really
love him!* Alas, not much I can do
about it." Mystery of the brass bound
trunk with Ron's papers. And today in
ARK I turn to the part about the
grave, O
save me for
the grave who
all the night make I my bed to swim

O
lion, compass
turn
to an end but arrows sing

They speak tongue tried in a furnace of earth,
on every side
I sleep the *sleep of
all*, not
one.

Rebecca and I are true *Wieners* now: eating Sachertorte & *schlag*, hot sausages, going to concerts, taking long walks in the Vienna Woods . . . [P. O'L]

VENUS. I who am the Queen of Love stand by, powerless, while he, my son, and she, the girl some called "Venus II," lie locked and chained in the powerful transport of love.

PSYCHE. I can't breathe . . .but what is breath? I never cared to breathe.

CUPID. I can't think . . . but what is thought? Never had any truck with thought.

[PSYCHE *and* CUPID *perform enraptured Bolero-type sex dance while Venus continues to sing, and invisible servants enter and mass around her.*]

"Nowadays in San Francisco it's just
fuck, fuck, fuck. I hate men! They're so
over," Nate tells me. Stood up by FedEx
guy, who wants to bring over whole "hordes
of men" to have sex while NL watches
I just spent $80 on your ass & you're gonna
tell me you

rose petals in water glass
Principe

Dodie meets Mac for a Barber concert
at Herbst Theater. Strange quiet night
cool fog, on the street, a whisper, hey
homeboy, we stare, the boy smiles wide, his
mouth is filled with brown vials
capping every other tooth, hey, homeboy
I'm walking her halfway there
down the concrete corridor to Van
Ness and Market. Frenchmen
love Cole Swensen: she's so thin and she's
got that haircut . . .

"Si t'etais beaucoup plus mince, Cole,
tu serais comme tes cheveux, ou plus mince,
tes cheveux fins d'or."

Imaginary Frenchman with
bright red coat and small cap. And what is
with Madonna's new Ray of Light
pre-Raphaelite processed hair, all that
scalp showing in between? It
feels like a New England hurricane's
blowing in, the sultry, expanding
air almost bursting with mist, but hot,
sweaty, the dishes won't dry.

VENUS *(bitterly)*. Look, invisible servants, on this, my mask of beauty,
here worn cold as stone in this eyeless palace of night.
It shines! Great beauty shines, yet like the silver moon
eclipsed by the sun's pale orange, it disappears
under the greater force of a children's game.

SERVANTS. Round and round like a child's game tumbles the earth, fair
ball of blue and white, and with it tumbles the sex of this world

Harsh like a ball of red fire, burning each as it goes

Desperate enough to kill a queen, it is the ruling passion of our planet,

And young enough for a boy and girl, and tots of all ages

We, the servants of mighty Cupid, are the toys in his box

He scatters us on the floor in poses ungainly and rude

and when he is done, his mother comes to the bedroom's threshold and
stares

coldly, as if she were not the Queen of love and beauty.

VENUS. Come, jealous sisters of Psyche, investigate like two Nancy
Drews,
sow the seeds of discord in your sister's heart.
Make her suspicious, make her a crone,

she is too young and lovely like a clover flower.
Wither her fresh vale and dry it like thrash.
What are these strange drops of blood
on the body of
Jennifer?

after James Schuyler & Ronald Johnson
RIP Ronald Johnson

Fiat Croma

He was here one minute, and now
I lie about him, day and night, now
His clothes are pinching
Lobster claws of the dead, while
all the kids are hip

There are no bruises, only KS lesions,
invisible scars in each cell, so the
giant white shot of kelatin
breaks down the resistance
cause it wouldn't be right

to leave your best girl home
and one minute, he was here, cracking
jokes and tails, and the next
I'm clutching the elementary clothes
of the grave, the shroud of

Pinche no? I get bugged driving
up and down the same old strip,
and they leave us alone, striking
the tension, pill after pill so that
you hate Evian water, my

lips are chapped, my feet are bright—
some kind of athlete's foot they
give to these guys, who never did anything
athletic in their *lives*, it's like
this *bonus Fiat Croma*

Probability Zero

Talking to my friend Emily, whose drinking

the corpses change but the party goes on forever,

flat tax soars while it's true, I haven't yet seen vaccine

In the interim he's puffing up, like a large green bullfrog

on the lily pad of the hospice, wet eyes yellow and glaucous

burning holes through the visitor

Probability zero, but don't let a sordid fatalism

give you that Monica Lewinsky fifth amendment

until there's a cure, but from what deep pockets

docs the money appear   When you're sick, the last

thing in the world is

Fit, the false falls into place, but sick

I don't know, but an erratic passion blows into our world

and I wilt a little, like figgy pudding

I don't know, where was I when everyone else I know

was getting bushwhacked, the bullshit of Clinton

In America, the probability's zero,—like weather,

like the inane weathermen on TV who tell you a

hot front and a cold front are moving into

a clearing, where I could be my "self,"

rituation normal

all fucked up, rnafu, or a "system is moving in"

and we're supposed to feign interest or terror—

while "watching" the "weather"

as years ago Tim died, the man who, whom

I once thought the FALCON MALTESE of sophisticated

and he did not love me but I was not worthy

His black glasses shiny like something alive,

the way that men do,

the way cattle do. He had a vision

I longed to share. His body was not so

pre

possessing. Probability zero that I would live

and he, Tim, his student ID the cover on his book,

would study death before I got to do him

I like felt this stab in my head

a red explosion of blood vehicles, brain flack,

infinitely painful as little by little he

always integral to my sense of myself

as a possible poet began to disintegrate

away across the wide border red ribbon swath of the US

away from me and, in time,

away from kissing him 1979

ten minutes later he spotted a rainbow

even then hoary cliche of gay experiential camaraderie

but, yikes, real—thin ribbon over Brooklyn

Look away, look away

this stormy river

after Tim Dlugos and in his memory

The Black Cat

Lucky cat, pets are people too,
          when you stroke me I wonder, God, what about that FIV?
—the HIV cats come down with . . .

                    Come cuddle with me while it rains, a black, tropical
                              rain here,
                    in the silver city

Tell me . . . with your paws tap out whose bones are piled
          on the inside of that dark drywall
wet now and stained with the blood of him

          him whom I loved, whom I don't know if,
                    if those old bones
          might once have lived inside his castle of

                    The castle of his skin, proud and stupid
                              moving in manifold directions, away
                    away from me, black cat, tell me . . .

          tho' FIV slows your taps to pats, free me up
                    out of this castle of him where he flew for cover,
          then slowly, dot dot dot

"K"

He kissed me, he is not worthy, to join the
KSW, and so is a slow
kick in the head, I will soak him
in kiwi fruit lube for his nasty
Klinefelter's syndrome*

"Knowing me, knowing you," un-hunh
keep his kerry off of my
Kidderminster, will you, his
knuckleball endures, his
kohlrabi wilted in my
little kitchenette, when he

kissed me, and it felt like a
keynote address, he
killed me, his swollen kestrel
in my keg—of ketchup brand beer

I'm not worthy of his
constant kelp, the ketone shining in his
kangaroo pouch, give me strength
kind sir, or the kilt of his
kinsmen

I'm living in his regard
His kumquat is my Picard, he
kissed me and it felt like
kimchi in a kiln

* The severe shrinkage of testicles due to abuse of ketosteroids.

Tenebrae

The poetry was in the gore, but in the American version the gore was cut out. Flat. How could these wet souls not love seeing through the specular glass? The blood, spattered over the kitchen cabinets.

Daria Nicolodi, a woman with a flip and a face as long as California, her raincoat flapping in the dark wind. Blue and magenta shadows bleed like what's not there. What happened?

Red stiletto heel in the raw mouth of the youth. The beach becomes a book, becomes a murder. I want to write a poem as long as California. "I didn't do it! I didn't do it!" Her body hurls through the plate glass, shards of undoing, dark pulsion glinting, the body unwound. A thousand holes like seeds, here in the seedy part of Rome. She takes a dagger in a darkroom, O heart of mine.

Revision. Victims emerge from the bath, unsane. I can't see their faces, but their sharp chemical beauty evaporates in the red air.

with Dodie Bellamy

I Can't Sleep

Udo Kier

The boy, dead on the forest floor:
rough tongue of deer licking his face, salty as sugar.
Spindly legs of deer, spindly as origami:
his body, wasted and angry in death.
Who is that boy, Rick Jacobsen, why do I see his face
lying still, pale, in the forest glade?
Overhead a bland ceiling of green leaves, sun poking through
Onto the glade of black, gritty dirt, pine smell.

"Rick Jacobsen, this is Udo Kier."
Rick Jacobsen, his red hair stained with sap and mousse.
Deer stand on spindly legs counting his freckles,
His corpse found awkward in baggy ACT UP style shorts, big shoes,
unlaced:
rich clothes fit over angry thin body,
human body now food for a forest of foragers.
Big owl in treetop high, hoots out his name, "Red boy,"
signalling four-legged predators. Red in tooth and
claw-footed they stagger like walking tables;
in silence they approach, not to honor the dead
but to shorten the world, thumping the floor
at midnight, so that by daybreak,
Jesus, you see all these deer licking his face.

Tongues pry open his pale eyelids slightly:
Rick's blue eyes blank but filled with green sun, forest light
where Ernest Hemingway prowled these big woods
where I introduced Rick to Udo Kier
giggle
the mad giggle of Udo Kier trying to speak English at a party
at Brett Reichman's opening at Rena Bransten gallery
and he signed my autograph book
he wrote that he loved me

Up in country outside of Wisconsin
with a big dog, the body heaves
tumbled aside by bear and game, outside of law.

His dirty face, now clean and wet, now streaked with mud;
his eyes and mouth jewels on the floor of the forest,
till, barrel first, a gun pokes between the trees

Udo's not so bad, not a bad shot
like masters, the deer go down, one by one
like falling trees down go the deer
If I did love thee in my master's stead
with such a gamy grin, my lips pulled back in rictus,
I would not understand it,
in my denial thou would see no sense

Cat o' Nine Tails

Karl Malden is blind, a girl of ten
leads him in the dark

Karl Malden blind, he creates crossword puzzles
outside the juridical system

Because the NEA is dead his
dick is ten feet long because
the gene runs rampant in his member
the dick of life, clumsy manifesto
to follow my tails of causing this, that
the other
On the rooftop I turn to you
and think,
I could push him off the roof

then a second thought scatters me like
like parsley

green dry freckles scattered in the
Washington wind, parsley flakes

Scott O'Hara died, the tattoo "HIV +"
bright on his shoulder
so you would know, so he would
inspire Sex Panic
not much of a writer, a video star
so Mark said, at Orphan Andy's, do you
actually know him, he's famous

now locked in the tomb
with Karl Malden, sharing cold cocoa, muttering

The cream it freeze, a muddy brown and gray on
top of the cocoa

Every tail pales compared to the elders
—push him under the gray wheels of that moving train

I'm looking askance and the evil cat
follows my gaze with yellow

Is there evil in the ways and making of man
I believe that out of a biological
warfare experiment gone wrong

US

Suspiria

I know when he began to dance with me
cranberries started to burn in pocket—
I smelled red smoke of sugar under my
feet, sugarfoot, a boy worth burning for—

and into his pants I'd push my white hands,
deeper into the sweeter red currant
in a darkened cell until he was done;
then into a lit cell, where I was king

if music played we sat down fast, out, down
into the red fruit mashed in my lap like
Turkey. Musical chairs with the pilgrims
who came here on the rock to fuck him good

Oh Bill, if you were living at this hour
I'd put little socks on your two bare feet
and spoon this dressing into your wet throat
till you choked and spat all over my bib

I'd give you such a gift of red white meat
you wouldn't be able to sit for a week
unless to eat at the mantelpiece with clock,
bawling pilgrims thrusting your ass with fire

ferret teeth in the breast of a red bird

I would call it to your memory now
that a phantasmal fog of love had enthralled me to you

then, but not only then, in these my words
the tear in the fabric, now, *the drop of blood.*

House of Wax

Her spooky face is bent
under the twisted apple blossom.
She takes your hand and gives it a wee squeeze,
awake, you scatter her ashes under
the twisted apple blossom.

"We're nothing but lab rats,"
she gasped,
drugged tubes piercing up her throat, like thorns,
leaky thorns, twisted brambles
but pure and white and red.

Men pull her toward the morgue.
Under the stinging white lights of the ray
techie type gowns hold out hands of salt
refresh us, they beg, in the house of
wax, the melting wax her body makes.

Give me back her floating eyes
I'll put them in my shadow box
and build a new face around them
smiling and screaming
mouth open, apple blossom falling from it
come on and let it snow

Il Tram

for Dennis Cooper

There are six of us on this tram
before we get to Minna Street
one of us will be murdered!

First I was Invisible Girl
then Wonder Woman
and now I am Thief Catcher

And who are you, she firmly spoke
When men fly over your
head I'm hatcheting ratcheting

Copy your sums
onto the ancient oaken bar
separating public from private tram riders

and pay your piper
Necklace of pearls
Lost down the piano wires of big Italian tram

Playing music as it approaches
our little alley
and the killer strikes glissando

Invisible Girl can you see him
Thief Catcher snatch his rat ass up
let's bar B Q him on Minna Street

Cough up those pearls
his wounds plugged with pearls
which when removed are washed

Asia Argento thinks she sees
someone she saw in the tram
humble down cobbled alley

no cloak but the night
his pearl like face a ghost face glow
over his shoulder as I snatch

up his rat ass
I copy my sums on said rat ass
breaking down wall between public

I don't know how you feel
about Ewan McGregor said Dennis
but after watching *The Pillow Book*
you get bored with his perineum

Testimone Oculare

"I saw something important that I can't remember"

Trailing the earwig
in one ear and out the other, too late
it's laid eggs, they crack apart
inside the slowly pumping brain

Conventions of horror demand a nut,
eyewitness, whose eyes can't be trusted,
but the life I've lived—gross,
the deracinated heart, pumping dully on a lead table
keeps faithful record of the life I've lived

The tortured, the abused, the égaré,
the lonely and eclipsed, the lost
Edina says to June, "I'm taking recovered
false memory therapy, I'll get something on you yet!
You in a hood in a wood—

it's all coming back to me now," on
Absolutely Fabulous. I saw something
important that I can't remember, for
the eyes wear no face, no memory strand

while inside the brain the earwig twins
grow in the dark, luminescent, toasty.
One vigorous shake of the head
should kill them, but "I want you to be:
volo ut sis," as Augustine said

for Avital Ronell

The Flowering Face

He read all his poems twice, thinking,
"they did not hear them the first time."

They hired a team of gay men who do this
gardening gig to do it for them.

If his body rots in the mouth of maggots
let's go to Zuni

Down his throat
poured a river of beer and rum

In the coercive moonlight of Diamond Heights
his red hair, gold

He'd like the symbolism
and of course the spring flowers

He was subtle, always said, "Hello my friend,"
as though he knew us better than indeed he did

If the words I wrote, and throw up into the sky, in his direction
mean what I think they do

Then deep into the black earth a post I dig, that says
retention must be paid

I found out who he really was
through the name on the bracelet, pink and white beads

A couple of guys from Ireland
passing through town and one says, "Die faggots"

If there was no poetry there would be no
toy, face, torment, healing, gladiola, prix fixe, heaven

Scott Street

And when I turn and you are not here
Only a habit, like cyclamen, to
turn to the sun

Goodbye dear, you are not for me,
You have turned at last into the sun
like moss of glassy green, a wave

But it was just one of those things
"The butterfly, my soul grown weak"
over the lamp, a green cloth

Moss dripping in shade
                                        twilight here
Moss past the moon, to tear away the

Wax from your chest, each tiny
hair screaming. If when I turn
To you as so often in the pasture

And you are not here, I've got a
new kick   he works as a waiter
in the restaurant on Scott Street.

This shiny tip I might have left for
you I hand to him to ensure proper
service and to get him high.

He's coming up the stairs, I suppose,
to take away the broken-hearted
memories of your coated black tongue

Needle sharing programs
dictated by Uncle Sam here on
the corner of Scott and Prince
in San Francisco back porch

The poem never says what lives in the barrel,
clear as his green eyes, no mirror
for the drug we ingest

Always a shot to the blood,
condom, dripping over the edge of cracked toilet seat,
mossy green and hacked up from your chest

In your final memory, I suppose
Why not?

We live under its law and
You died and he's pounding up the stairs
like his hair's on fire and his ass is catching
Oh Johnny, women in the night
call out yr. name

after John Wieners

Inferno

Inferno maybe too descriptive
I lived with him for seven years
black under water, a shark on fire

Are you the patient XYZ?
who blew smoke up my ass
and fell into watery aphrodite loving me!

Rip that tube from the wall and feel me up
loving you and forcing you to wriggle a bit
a sausage on griddle, hot

Mother of tears, mother of shadows
give him a little more zip
I don't want him self-conscious
when he walks among dot dot dot

Big, bright colors like a Cibachrome painting
by Nan Goldin should she turn to oils.

I ate the seventies dancing in disco
and made the eighties this fresco experience
Now I'm impoverished, begging

for my birth mark, going on thorazine
should I turn to oils, shark under fire
or should I just say, *tattoo man, make*

me a birth mark, say it was me from the
beginning, and in thy honor I shall
do thee justice? I lived with him when he

died and I'll live when he abrades me
for he is the Saxon justice of a women's
barony, he gives me strength, to carry on

he lights up my life, disco inferno
night falls on a prodigal landscape, loving
him was never light mechanical

Mother of mercy, mother of pain
tell him for me he lives on my derma
when I pull it off gently after the chemo

He won't love me without my foreskin
tiny little snip of waxwork
only a storm toss'd frigate by Turner

Tell him there's some easy pickings
long and low the banks of the Mersey
white Jersey daisies and calla slips

creeping up the inner side of his leg
locks and curl then up to inside his anus
where I admitted the thorazine early

Mother of HIV, mother of envy, grant me
the shallow wish to be loved like a man
in the highest way, la vita nuova, in your

shallow dish I shall take to Goshen
learning the ropes inefficient way, if the
boat don't break don't fix it, miles of

ash and fire all you can see, in your throat,
your naked silver throat, a shallow boom
box, glug, it's coming through and we're

history.

Unsane

> CHARLES: Your behaviour has shocked me immeasurably,
> Elvira—I had no idea you were so unscrupulous.
> ELVIRA (*bursting into tears*): Oh, Charles . . .
> CHARLES: Stop crying.
> ELVIRA: They're only ghost tears—they don't
> mean anything really—but they're very painful.
> —Noël Coward, *Blithe Spirit*

Anyway it was only because I loved you—that's right
So rub it in what high hopes I started out with. Okay
A nightingale
does sing
outside this window

Trying to live my regular life
Touched in the head, a wand exploding on my hairline
Look! I'm 44, I've come through
Okay, so there's now a knock at the door for you
my love
With trepidation you answer it

His face is carved from anthracite
His body cloaked in protease inhibitor
So, net result is, can't see the fog for the trees
Oh dear, but that is what happens
in the Canadian century
sip of water from wet canteen

that I rub over your face, pick up sweat, tears,
and the incorruptible eschatology
of the book you devoured,
kins,
a girl worth a million of two thousand boys

I'm unsane, my books are parked on 101,
a bird at the window pecking
hard cold beak-like nose, I'm under your weather
in romantic Cancun . . . blue field,
rose stripe

Agnes Martin, her paintings must go for
400, 500 thousand, living in
immaculate motor court and studying the
patterns of PBS in the dark quiet Taos night
nearby the mausoleum of Lawrence. You

can see I've been trying to get through to
the dead ones—a pierced veil, who broke ranks, *the act of*
a generous heart. The city fritters in
fear, of the unsane, approach him with gloves,
you needn't come down like a ton of bricks

Okay, a masked creature does
approach the window on Jones Street in
San Francisco, the town without graveyards—
Stymied by your willfullness, I trace
the rim of a beer mug on your beer face.

They don't mean anything really:
the tears, the sweat, the semen, that
flow incorruptibly from the faces of Mary,
but they're very painful.
Slouching at this bar helps me work, I swear.
Stymied by your mouth I bite off your hair.

after Robin Blaser

Creepers

Night, and they walk unsane, sprawling chins of steel,
the fearless, the torn, the lamentable . . .
freaks of the underworld.
                                        Warm misty moon
high above landing on Minna Street
once a bordello, now
black rubber curtains part . . . to unveil
a silly beer bottle, like a genie, in a bottle,
twinkling with smoke and pink fluid . . .
                    always the unsettling memory of
moonlight, sharp and sudden.

                                                  When
you were very young, studying TV,
space people go into Mars as boldly
as the creepers who crawl my street . . .
shoes in their mouths, shoes
          in their mouths so no one can scream at them.
                                    I've got a line open
waiting by the phone and nothing but
          the bad news of every day
warm misty moon, unseasonable
heat for February, like a scarlet sno-cone
those freaks of the underworld . . .

TV's warm, as though someone
had helped a stranger.   His body,
turned facing the set, tuned to TV,
nineteen stab wounds closing with clotted blood, and vermouth . . .
in an interlingo of clicking glottal stops . . .
and his hands move to the screen, as though the stranger had turned
  into a
friend.
          "Hello" in English.
Master puppeteer, rods twitching

strings jumping, and the tiring thing is the thing we must do first
sunlight or no, moonlight or no . . .
I'm no expert, though I wish I was, I was more like a man,
in this tiny apartment
living from week to week,
                                                            until the steps
on my forty stairs, like thieves, stop,
hold a finger to their teeth, and clamp
on your old brown shoe, a cat in heat.
                                          . . . If I give you my whistle,
you'll yawn . . . your mouth so open
you could suck on it dry as heaves, scary, like some kind of—
—pus freaks of the underworld—
                                          street goon stabbing you nineteen
times for money, in your neck and face

Larry Eigner, Bob Flanagan, you guys
were kind of sick before you died, huh?
              Air creeps through the lungs, the tiny
                            sore branchials, thievery internet
with no return, up my forty steps
you just stop there dead—I don't want to
with diseases I saw on TV and in the stores,
              tugging on Dad's sleeve whispering, what is
it with those people, Dad? Warm moonlight misty with lotion
on my hands, I see these guys
on the Jerry Lewis Telethon, and two of them
were you. Wheels of a cart
trundle down the stairs to
the alley   the heap of cracked bones

creep down my street, once a bordello,
you two men, flesh rotting off your bones
like tenderized shrimp in the market
always remembering and seeing
              when the clouds disperse
I whistle across the great warm wind like a bunch of creepers
                            to wriggle up the steps under my door

into my bed and night dreams
        the seven orifice body loving me for what I am
since you came to California for my birthday, "Oh!
Man! This is *unsane!*"

Cemetery without Crosses

Things are fine
with me—good writing,
good fucking—Ideal really

Pyramids
to be arranged
in the shape of a cross

Americans
cut up the four hour
Trauma

He's not
so spectacular, I
mean, I'd do him but

And he
is Ronald Johnson
a far cry

How dare
you write me of
fucking somebody else

Valencia Street
rain on your face
ravaged, ruined blood face

O lion, compass
turn
to an end but arrows sing

made
all the dishes
from one of his cookbooks

and he is
Ronald Johnson
name the date

Four Flies on Gray Velvet

Il Marchio di Nascere:
the old dead family heirloom, watch closely as
          Mimsy Farmer, a blond kitten with an American backhand
one more box with me, Mimsy pleads
                    in the dying arms of the old box pedlar

Non! He sings with a kind of visionary rapture
tucking cats into sandwiches for the poor
          people of Rome—*Non!* She plays her trump,
a perfect circlet of guitar hole for the masses,
                    he eyes it needily, oh Mimsy, shame!

for you are rich as velvet in the gray matter
while he's needy, though what a tenorous bagpipe of love,
          can't you have spent your largesse in a different light? Take
the old surgeon of Rome, he's poor as four flies,
                    cradling the enormous *Marchio di Nascere*

while you hack away and blame the stud husband
whose only crime is snooping through demesne.
                    Box man shakes his black and white, sorry
but—No! His famous aria, "Non!"
          Not in a million years, Mimsy Farmer!

In a way too bad, since you are only the victim
of a rapacious dad and absent woman thing who cared
                    but couldn't cut the mustard, while the very three-
dimensionality of characters doom them
          to moody baby doom a yam, etc.

As one by one, the men I knew and loved, or disliked
leave this planet due to a rapacious virus
                    my widow wear gets lots of use
in the middling funeral march hare nightmare
          that's the way of our times, I know, but

how can I keep going, tell me, Mimsy Farmer
the weakness of support, the get well cards unsent
                    saquinavir trickles into vein like syrup
the insipid drain of hospital white, wash your hands
          how to keep from screaming as one by one

Ammonia wreaks their joints, a look alike
and death looks more like a person than he used to
                    look at me, under the fringe of hair
Or over the raggy edge of an old book of old Foucault theory
          when I had my jacket on, black leather,

gray velvet. When I walked into the crowd, forgetting
my fly was open, and you lingered behind me, pointing
                    I have been embarrassed again
by my genitals' behavior, and how they once peeked
          into the face of a world-wide epidemic etc.

yet a cat can look at a king, in the films of Dario
Argento, and way to go, Mimsy Farmer for your
                    sterling performance in his
strange fever. Nasty patches on my epidermis
          like four flies, on gray velvet, but nothing

La Setta

The thing described makes a run for it

to the form of the question

Say you were in a cult as a girl

would memories haunt a woman, repressed

The panting footsteps of the thing, described

a faery ring,

the OK corral, hung with Cady Noland-type

memories of Manson

until blanched hands rip from out of red sand

the swirling tumbleweeds

and tackle your face in a patchy Italy

needles ring your face like Oberon, a tingle

your face rips off, later

a stud shows his face and a scream

runs ribbons around the world, the thing

described six hundred feet tall,

and pretty ugly

Today It's Me—Tomorrow You!

The Inn of the Red Leaf

Robert Duncan: Sonnet 3: From Dante's Sixth Sonnet

Robin, it would be a great thing if you, me, and Jack Spicer
Were taken up in a sorcery with our mortal heads so turnd
That life dimmd in the light of that fairy ship
The Golden Vanity or *The Revolving Lure.*

Whose sails ride before music as if it were our will,
Having no memory of ourselves but the poets we were
In certain verses that had such a semblance or charm
Our lusts and loves confused in one

Lord or Magician of Amor's likeness.
And that we might have ever at our call
Those youth we have celebrated to play Eros
And erased to lament in the passing of things.

And to weave themes forever of Love.
And that each might be glad
To be so far abroad from what he was.

Bring in the prisoner
in black and white telephones, shackles
he will tell what he knows of the red inn of the red leaf
if I am a judge of men

"It's in Canada"
Is that all you can tell us, prisoner of the
black jail in Milan winter?

My tongue torn away by plants
emits a wig and wag, that's all, c'est Leonor fini

The Inn of the Red Leaf
slap his face

make him cough up in blood more details
not just "it's in Canada" do you think us fools!

In the winter of my 45th year
I was on the phone with Dodie
and she said Kathy Acker was very sick

The white washed walls of the police state office
and the sweat of the prisoner
talking without crosses
supported in the chair and thinking these thoughts
with no direction

Who went to Venice, the icy banks of the canal
Who went to Tijuana on the wings of a snow white dove,
now you see her, now you don't
Ahora la mira, y ahora no
Waiter! Check into the inn of the red leaf
Accommodate party of large egos with
utmost civility
On New Year's Eve
I'm sitting here thinking, where is she now

Dodie, I would like it if you and I and Kathy Acker
Were all still alive through some Jamaican voodoo herb
And our Filipino healer put us on the fairy boat
like *Pussy King of the Pirates* but with less pressure

A big ship with a white sail that thrills to loud music
And we could not remember who had written what
and who had stolen what passage from another
"our lusts and loves confused in one"

like Harold Robbins filibustering with red face in UK courtroom—
And I'd like it if all the fellows we ever loved
And been dominated by before pirate advent
And the men who died so that we could live and sail

Kind of, you know, were like the slave boys.
And I'd smile to you and you and she at me
To be on this funny sea, this choppy cool violet water.

Goblin

I'll have the glass, the shimmering dust
to see the ragged real better
through its shade
and second skin
—Charles Watts, "Dramatic Realism"

I keep waiting for a break, alas—
ten thousand party favors have to be blown up and placed,
just so,
on the table of the zombies of the lake

"Of the," "of the," all this possession
I'm haunted by, built into the structures of English
like that shadow on the dinette table

It is hundreds of years old, and creaks with yellow

Watts up Charlie Chan? I used to say
on the telephone, can I put you on hold,
slamming down before he could say yes or no,
"Now I'm back," but you never know
if the distant person will be there still
breathing

a ferocious guess
the ragged real, and I would say
what's so real
we're just molecules who went to school

Each dust point's a blazing prism
the glass a crystal screen
and cast against the glamor
the image, vine and leaf,
of blackberry,
whose body, almost unleaved, thick, still

unwithered, green and armed,
endures the February light a foot away.

I'm afraid of my face, that gathers in a scrunchie
all of the sights I witnessed in a trance
A round robin of sights
that, once eaten, never graduate
from the Tanz Akademie of Joan Bennett, Alida Valli
& what is that thing that looks
like a giant slinky
try to escape it, your flesh tears off in liver strips?

Kill a bat, light a cigarette, breathe easy
except for the face pinned to one's skull
Watts up, Charlie Chan, I haven't
got all day
I'm a busy man
More peccable than the boy, still unwithered,
armed, green, the unendured
and a foot away from il lago di zombi . . . darkness

The Stendhal Syndrome

With a rush, and we do away
Look at those Brice Mardens
and the big horses of Susan Rothenberg
and the palette without color of Neil Jordan

Pleasure as a synonym for AIDS
its metonymic attachment to the body
the fringe on top of the surrey of living
easy without you, easy air Jordan

Color my world white, with veiny streaks of red
A terror at giving up my seat at the opera
the family box
I really fucked myself over, that box of steak.

Steel stripes shadow the steel pier—Brighton
Smegma nada, the reverse of what?—My dick
tiptoes through the sands in another's—shoes
a river wide, green desert ribbon—

Opera

The tricky part is keeping your eyes.

Loving isn't enough, not with needles.

Overhead of the crowd beats the black crow,
His chance revenge.

Betty the teenage opera star in her
glittery black and silver Raiders gown
the crow, attentive, tilts his beak to caw
though no sound escapes

My mother slept with him long ago
Now he's back to give me an opera
dedicated to my name
in this theater holy with my death.
Unlucky love, that left to my devices
needed transfusion from lens to lens,
takes off his shirt in deco profusion
giving me head over hand over hand,
unlucky in love, lucky in cars
pull over and pick me up
I'll take you where

I've been watching you since
you were a child
In the corner of the schoolyard playing ball
and reading Wayne Koestenbaum

I've got a van with locks that shoot down into the doors, once you're in
head over hand over hand

Folly to take so limpid a face for a match
the gun droops from your pale hand

give me the gun, dear
I'll bind your green bruises with this ketone acetate,
that freezes into cloth once bound around
an itchy trigger finger

the swelling must go down

van back, cold corrugated metal, scrap of red carpet
put your eye to the keyhole
while the stitches force you to see
that which is unseeable
the collision of the ghosts in the hall
singing an aria, and banging into each other,
their flesh, not flesh, stinging then melting
they pass without speaking, only surprise
the tricky part is keeping your eyes
ghosts pause, behind each other now
do you see them in the dusty hall
see them shimmer, reading Wayne Koestenbaum
the crow, attentive, tilts his beak to caw
a sound escapes

Attention focused on the van
it starts to hump, to rock, its fat black tires
squeezing
and sighing, and swelling

Ink those tires, drive them over white strips of
paper like John Cage and Robert Rauschenberg

Like John "Van" Cage and Robert
"Van" Rauschenberg

The Door into Darkness

A hand within touching distance of the doorknob.
No light, no sound, the lintel black with absence and size.

The wristwatch that talks, "Time for your medications."
Feeling, the cold drip inside your thigh, the scent of fear.

Quiet, the set is cleared and the long spaces grow still, dark.
Bitter scent of attempted, the light, the warm hatching eggs.

Open the door, pick its hinges, flood the house with darkness.
A short burst of steam, the mailbox slot hot as his asshole,

darkness within and the field of the open human page. The
check for his pills, and a glass of water from crystal springs

tipped to his mouth: he is old now, yodelling in a sleep
indecent, cracked, his hand furtive sly yanks at a single sheet—

Pull at the tubes, throw open the black wooden door and let go.
All the world staring at him from inside his own eyes

and I'm like, the hand that takes the door by the knob, firmly,
uprooted, as once I made him come with my hand, till he

couldn't stop gasping for breath. Now he can breathe, now
he can live, now he can come, now he can write "dead" in the dark.

Bad Blood

When two people live in squalor
the dictator among us grins
His snigger subtle as gnome's fingerfuck
Rotting cicada,
imitation rolex worn at the elbow, like his aqualung
worn at the lung
like cough, reflexive cough of Allen Barnett

He's interesting for a year
then you tire of his what.

Did you ever think you'd be seeing him humbled
Not quite there, and even that is sad! Where's the party?
Always thought that maybe, if only, I'd turn on the lights
on the one boy, in the shape of melty copper, his fresh
underwear grinning at his waist in the window—
And now, in the afterlife of Nijinsky, a
mess of pottage I gave up my birthright to anagram:
He is the victor, defeated, spanked.

On the deck he naps, his sorry ass slung in my deck chair
Poetry Princess
from the civil tsi-tsieh of Kim Ki-young detached as dainty Rottweiler
Well, Sam, it took me ten years to
think of a way to return you from the grave
All bets are off now, we're sailing in an hour
Turn over his rolex to its backside, read its inscription, from Sam to
   Kevin 1988
and say it's not stolen, stripped from the bony arms drooping off the
   gray metal table—
I can read, can't I? I can be this kind of—
reading person—

KizZool cuz skiZool iz out ÷
It's cool ÷ cuz
school is out ÷

WOW did you ever see even in a museum
such a collection of boddisatvahs ÷ the way
the way they have to sit above the rubber

Or that one was, inside his pants, the Yiddish poet
a vegetarian. Or another—all in his mouth—a snarl
of the Sources. The one I loved most, who once,
once only, let go the pain, the night he got drunk,
and I put him to bed, and he said, Bad blood.÷÷÷÷÷÷÷÷

after Charles Olson

Trussardi Action

Shadow, dart away, let me be, with invisible scissors cut me some slack,
I'm so tired of your trespasses, dark shape that moves in my body—
Lithe and shapely, attractive, wow.
Everywhere I walk, a chill runs across my path like a black cat on fire
Never to be mastered or shifted, here's to whistling in the dark
Clever chill that knows which way I'm coming
Everywhere I walk with you, shadow man.

Even as we speak you're imitating the way I talk
Quarrelling with me by using my gestural pneuma
Under the twisted apple blossom, a shadow falls, not of this earth
And even as I try to have sex with somebody else, you're
Like a virgin
Shut away for the very first time

Dark boy, playing with yourself, contorting my body
Everywhere I go, I'll make you shiver, you'll regret this impertinence
As you follow me, I'll be wearing Trussardi
The clothes of another country, woven from light
Here in the art of another your hands will be forced from my dick
And bound behind your back, your eyes closed
My men will ready, aim, fire
Ho, ho, ho, Henry Higgins, just you wait!

Bullets pierce a shadow,
Hit a wall, that I got to see. Without my assistance you
Couldn't find my ass with both hands, if that's what you call them.
Shadow condensed of the dozens, go now,
Me to live in a world of lanterns, flashing grief from each pore in my
Real body, while yours lies, dead harlequin,
On the black and white carpet of action Trussardi.

Daria

If I had a lira, beyond the Aegean
as you were floating on a dolphin's tail,
salt, silver, your eyes closed to the heavy sun
and I were a transvestite, wearing
the clothes of a woman and the red
high heels of death—
If you didn't like the sex, you had only
to say so many words so glibly, dog-paddling,
I put the headphones on your ears
simultaneous transmission to
the States and to Canada, where
the corn grows higher, and corner, so
if you were my woman and I was
a man, sinking deeper under the dolphin's
funny genitals, into a blue empyrean ringed
with coral cacti and flibbertigibbets
as my grandmother used to say—
what's goose for the gander?
If I were a king and Daria, you could be my
favorite star, the tainted goddess
I wanted to be as a "grown up"—young,
young forever in the house I was born in
only to be yours, lost, rapt, a pretty girl
in heels to bust my eyeballs. Always think-
ing I'd escape from your love—as you;
Sinking, or thinking, could I be you?
Nonetheless you'd leave, me to your card
stained with mud, dark souvenir
of the UFA we both knew as an arid skin
sloughed off in the arid bath of my tears

Who

Who, I didn't love him enough
ninety thousand names for the government
to gamble on, to conjure, out of a hole
so big it could be only

Who said to me *look at my lesions, no,*
Kevin, really look, don't look
at the stars
enough of your avoidance behavior

His body, in state, or tumbled through
a rinse cycle drying in the feathery wind
lint on your net, your intersticed
net, who
I loved so long but not enough

Who gave Steve Abbott the "AIDS Award
for Poetic Idiocy" seven years before he died?
(Ed Dorn)

Who, rather than waiting
seized his little liver in a
silver thimble, the man I mistook for a moulting
hen, I, reigning the roost, the big cock of 1983,
I
impenetrable safe of steel, those
tiny fingers made me look like a monkey

Who on the plush row
of velvet embroidery, Joni Mitchell sobbing
in the pew behind me, "I wish I were a river
I could skate away on," a thirst so deep
confession doesn't cover it

I wanted him to live
to fill his throat with "Mela, mela peto

In medio flumine," but who
was it told me
They are moving his body
into the memorable room of a long love

Who was the mad man who took him back,
while we watched indignant such a man could go
in the front row with Lisa and Dan
watching David Wojnarowicz scream
his spittle on my chin
at the gay bookstore in San Francisco

marvelling at, comparing him,
who did this to me, that I
lived and did so little to be clear
always the quaint uppermost in mind,
my mad strive for personality,
always the quaint peppermint misread
who

made the little tiger the big lamb on Sunday,
broke my will, gave me to the boy
following him down to the grave
holding back, something
ungiven

who launched this rocket into space,
that burst into earth, one death at a time,
its rockets a flare of red and pink pinspots,
livid bouquet in the night sky
over beautiful city
whose garden did I pick this death from?

Zing, zing, a phone insistent
as kismet, the fate that brought me to
a dark reply, hello, is Kevin Killian
home, I've got a message, and
who is this, I whisper into the phone,

who did you say was calling
for him, the straight black mouth
of the plastic phone,
I'll see if he's in
and who did you say, if you did say

and I don't think you did say
who, who took me to this
date in my history, who made my
feet scatter like the burnt leaves of
the oak seedlings, while I walk to
the phone as though nothing
were happening,

under the sky, under the rain, in San
Francisco, home of the birds and the
sun and the big bottle of dilaudin and
morphine I gave to him Sunday
and leaving him, quietly, I closed

the door on my nation

Zombie

Father who keeps one great yellow eye peeled for the
Boy, don't let him grow up to be that peeping Tom
With the German accent. Father of definition, let no

Glaucoma take him behind the screen of white china,
He's my little wriggling thing I eat like a jujube.
Out of your mouth you spewed me like catfish, lukewarm,

Whiskered, "hot diggety dog!" said the other children
Crowding round my genitals as though on Bonfire, but
Then coming back to school to pray, heads bowed

Father who makes this body of sense go stupid
Whenever I see you burning in that berry bush,
Keep your guard down till over your self-defense I leap.

I once did ooze, but now I'm hard, I'll become lard
If a prayerful sort. Dance class at noon, I expect
Every *Mein Herr* to take that duty, dinner at sevenish,

Little gummy green bear assails us at table with news of
Thee, soup on the left, big bowl of snapdragons floating
In the water of Thee. Dear God, as I lay dying of AIDS

I prayed to you and all your ministries nightly and daily,
And you were out in school teaching us the colors of the fag.
Dear God, let me freeze up his serious T-cells into miasma

And bring him alive in the 23rd century, I can't lose
Everything—not in 1 day. Jesus fucking Christ, I'll bring
Corpse after corpse to wash your feet with, to open a closet

With a bullet in space, sleep if you are tired, rest if
You feel trenchant. Father of HIV stop the digital maniplex,
Close your eyes, close your eyes, relax think of nothing tonight.

The Phantom of the Opera

Had this been a heterosexual these two boys decided to take out and rob, this never would have made the national news. Now my son is guilty before he's even had a trial.

His little feet are green.
Take the barrel off the wright
for his green feet. For a load of
chops. Matthew Shepard, 21
Propellor to the stars, the green stars, high over Laramie's
outskirts and weary and back to the base line
the fence on which they found him
a scarecrow

I fell apart when he approached,
a dizzy fog flailing round my skeleton
arms flapping, and used this
to write novels

the beautiful birds this dead boy scared away
the welts forensics took for burns

this weakness—
in intensive care
Nurse figures in transit, and swift about it
Doctor, stat,
have you ever seen feet so green
he's been stepping on clover
a piece of state scum

dunked into a barrel. Boys
said the queen of Minna Street
have you been set upon by thugs
Russell Henderson, 21
Aaron McKinley, 22,

themselves slight,
who robbed you of your underwear

Boys don't forget me
I've your welfare at heart
said the queen of Minna Street
his pale feet in the rug of their scalp

As they walk away
their asses throb like chlorophyll
shrug

A is for Kevin
B is for missed the bus on O'Farrell Street, standing there, my paper
  and dick
C is for AIDS deaths dropped in half in 1997, now only the 15th killer
  in America
D is for plastic sheets, two men huddle beneath, dancing, performance
          and E is for the night we
saw Louis Malle and Uma Thurman in that restaurant
          and met Kiki Smith

"F," as in Clint Eastwood, hairy stare
          K to the I to the double-L
anagram = Old West action, what do they spell

Matthew Shepard, 105 pounds, five foot two,

"G,"—other causes leap out of the pack
          accident, suicide, murder, sign of the cross
                    as AIDS drops down to 15
                              after 15 years
and murder in Laramie
          "A" is to axe and "H" is to hatchet
"I" is for "iris" and "J" is for "jacket"
He took a long turn to 405,
kept the cure, his neck burnt black
"J" put the stopper in perfume X
took the wheat from the Blistex bottle

"K" for the almost perceptible slur
in your bankbook, I don't remember half
of these guys, that got key-toned

Exist now as letters only—
alphabet mired in gum
"L" is for Matthew, who sat on a fence, scaring crows,
"M" did the wild thing on my dime

The pop art [George Oppen wrote]—a Disneyland tour of Dadism? or the anger, the destructiveness of the homosexual, the totally disconnected, the man without natural valences—to him not only the structure but the purposes of society must seem AT ALL MOMENTS totally absurd.

Black plantain cross rosary plate
on snowy white linen
snarled with your drool
so I keep my books in plastic sheets
I am the little boy who went in
            to the sea to rescue your scarf

from misery heap, picked over by
hungry—
and—
It is true, Christine

I am not an Angel, nor
a genius, nor a ghost

I am Erik

Forget the name of the man's voice

the corpses change but the party goes on forever,

Today It's Me—Tomorrow You!
(*Oggi a me . . . domani a te!*)

Gothic set-up for a dollar climax,
money comes into the room,
the candle disappears.
I'm AIDS'ed out, pockets turned back to front,
inside out, flapping like whitefish
in my white pajamas
We can be like they are . . .
Curse its gilded milkteeth! Dedicate the
grave to Nothing! In the camera's eye
my body moults from feathers
to a tough tensile steel,
reenacting the bird bath of another agent.
Romeo and Juliet
another 40,000 every day come
up the subway steps to New York
Tall gray buildings hot with light
and long rows of the hospital dead
There's a place I know
where we can go and have some coffee
nor do the wind, the sun and the rain
His tots cry around the relict
gorgeous music for a shapely eunuch
his tots now orphans, the ceiling
of paternity lifted off and swept to the
dark sky

Sucked clean, eh.
Out of the night, and just when the plink of sleep
falls out of the dollar
100 per cent down coverlet so cozy
white as fluorescence

A low roar, mounting, the mind alone.

"Seasons don't fear the reaper,
nor do the wind, the sun, and the rain,
we can be like they are."

it was an older man showed me
the steps of the dance
I can't forget
tall man whose shoes I
stepped on when
I was trying

to write
before AIDS catastrophe
made writing inequitable
the mind, alone, a corsage
of pink crinkles rather
like the asshole of Tommy
which when

I touched it with my thumb
wet
shivered alive, alcrt
in Port Jefferson
above a harbor ringed with boats
on the bed a web of his
wet clothes
that's me
thinking

Aura's Enigma

FOR JULIANA SPAHR

Aura's Enigma

Dear Juliana,

Dario Argento's *Trauma* begins with a Rumanian girl, played by the director's young daughter Asia, trying to jump off a bridge in downtown Minneapolis. Unlike Argento's previous heroines, "Aura Petrescu" comes with a lot of emotional baggage—perhaps because it's an "American" film—bourgeois conventions of characterization imposed onto a purer cinema? . . . She's escaped from the Faraday Clinic, she's suffering from bulimia, which the film treats as a visionary gift, like the (false?) mediumship of her mother, the grand European Piper Laurie, doing a great Grace Zabriskie imitation in gypsy shawls and jeweled hairpins.

Bulimia, the rush to evacuate, the ecstasy of revulsion, the insane thrust of the pure—counterpoised to the TV news world of Aura's new American boyfriend—the world which sucks everything in and is hungry for more, more info, more pictures, more drugs and sex. How unflatteringly photographed is Aura's rival, the older, jaded anchor-woman played by Laura Johnson! She's seen in bed in a dark room, yet a harsh strange light reveals tons of acne scars, while her lips move with vulgar inanities. Bulimia here is a mark of European cultivation and old world mystery, yet also as a uniquely American stigmata: as the pompous pal reminds us, "there are four million of these girls *in this country.*"

Naturally the casting of Piper Laurie as the evil mother calls De Palma's film of *Carrie* to mind. Every other scene in *Trauma* seems to be missing, but the music throbs on and on, like a sewing machine drilling a seam, a rhythm, into the scraps of plot. And oh those secondary characters! Okay, they're all victims, but they're kooky, vivid, "multicultural" in fact—escaped from an Altman picture, their lives the fluttery captivity narratives America serves up to the foreign cineaste like doughnuts.

Naturally it wouldn't be an Argento film without one of those "I saw something important I can't remember" elements to dig furrows of worry and loss into its heroine's smooth brow. Bulimia as escape from memory, and food as experience, the greasy diner food shared with the boy in reel one a revolting counterpart to seeing your mother dangle the head of your dad next to her face in reel two, in a dark thicket, with sheets of pink rain pouring down, a wood so dark and cold Oberon and Titania have fled it. The mad doctor who imprisons Aura in his clinic feeds her the magic berry juice from *A Midsummer Night's Dream* and all she can recall is her father leaning down to kiss her. "The bulimic may have recurrent dreams," the narrator tells us. "Her father will be leaning down to kiss her."

Half of event is therapy. The killer lives next door to a little blond boy who plays with insects; a butterfly watches him play and we see the boy from the butterfly's point of view. The boy follows the butterfly through the shuttered window of the killer's house, in broad daylight, and discovers the wooden box in which she stores the Noose-o-Matic. The Noose-o-Matic, slipped around the victim's neck, tightens a razor-sharp string when a button is pushed; kind of a portable guillotine, but very, very Black and Decker, and of course it's never explained how a woman of Piper Laurie's ancestry and dementia has the Rube Goldberg machine shop background to invent such a northern tool. We're not talking efficiency, for the Noose-o-Matic leaves its victims' heads messy on motel room floors, still gasping a last few words when discovered by police (like Z-Man, in Russ Meyer's *Beyond the Valley of the Dolls*). We're talking about how people talk after death, in the realm of Spicer's low ghost. The other half of event is trauma—you could cut my head off, I will still manage a talking cure; birth itself, in a hospital room in a power outage, can be traumatic; how about if your mother shackles you in a basement cage and clearly prefers your dead brother? Watching Argento makes one realize what a child one has always been and is always likely to remain, and how deeply one wants that child dead or snatched. Like the dulled, shocked witnesses of your UFO abduction poem, the child invariably draws the simplest conclusions from the surging tumult of culture. *I was taken by an alien intelligence. My food is trying to poison me. A serial killer is on a "rampage."*

Why take the heads anyway? I guess to give yourself an alibi or to plant them on the dupe mad doctor. Are all those heads going to give me back my Nicolas? I want to avoid having sex with my graphic artist boyfriend. I'll arrange it so my food spews out of me like ectoplasm as I race around the corner to the nearest public toilet—spilling in front of me, projectile as an erection, but fluid, dashed with light and color, like a lava lamp. In despair the child says, I'll do everything I can but it still won't be enough! Love,

Kevin

ACTION KYLIE

FOR DODIE BELLAMY

"To have every man but to love only one
To wake with the moon and sleep with the sun

These are the dreams
Of an impossible princess

Man and woman, boy and girl
They want to escape this world"

—"Dreams" (1997), written by Kylie Minogue,
Steve Anderson, and Dave Seaman

City Games

Slow

Brainstakingly the chimney sweep
prowling gets coat dirty and his goat
tethered, meowing, to the bricks of the chimney

It takes so long for the little
girl's tip off
goat's crying by then. Takes forever.

Gay men international
stand resolute shoulder to shoulder
hip to hip, in Barcelona pool, blue water

Can Emilíana Torrini do for Kylie
what Paula and Cathy have done in the
past, i.e., provide her with further comeback

fodder

Like the sooty games of the boy
up in the air
Victorian girl of the upper class nods so

discreetly, Master Commander of
schoolroom sees not the soot, hears not
the whining of tethered goat in

schoolyard   Slow
inkling of change

City Games

after Akira Kurosawa's Dreams *[1990], with Kylie Minogue*

Winning in the walking run
Any second now, I can't listen to this
shit

Clouds of organza, peach-colored, part
and suddenly Kylie is yakking in
Japanese, tortured by memories
of once she was in a

Yakuza . . . there are filaments
of fire so bright you can't put your
fingers on the screen

Copy to second screen
which, pixilated freely, you can punch
your face into it, feel the fever

Kylie meets old lady who looks
remarkably like . . .

Up on Mount Fuji US GI gives himself
to old lady, saving the world for dreams
Only 19 when "Dreams" was made, Kylie
shows remarkable poise in
brief tunnel sequence—

—*"Ninety per cent of the game is fifty per cent mental"*

Mother in jail, leaves tot "home alone"
survives on Fritos, jelly, educational talk shows
like Charlie Rose Giants win in
walking run, credits roll down to

walk in the sun and to have every man
and love only one—

"These are the dreams of an impossible princess."

You Make Me Feel

knowing, you make me feel
this trippy silent thud in my coccyx, spun sugar

Green grow the lilacs in traditional
old-time spinning wheel

reluctant colonial revival of my colon

Knowing you make me feel like
ball-crunching pull on parachute harness, the snap

of your lapels

Irresistible twitch of your little finger
at the bottom of the second inning
on steering wheel driving

prowling pet's coat's dirty and your cat
tethered, meowing, to the side of the catnip
doing this kind of Christina Aguilera
electric slide in your tube socks

Why you haven't laughed this hard
since Robert Palmer died

Second Thoughts (about the so-called opposites)

Fire on the one hand
Earth on the other

“On the one hand” itself a kind of death wish,
wizened fingers fumbling for the catch

“On the other hand,” like a school of pigeons
pecking for crumbs, rush alight when they see your shoes.

Shoes for style
Gloves, Cockney rhyming slang for style

As in “Wotcher, Bill, got any gloves?”
Second thoughts about letting you walk away

long legs storming off toward
Stork Club, fire in your one hand

(lit cigarette on chilly balcony, condo
windows squares of light across the lane)

and in the other, earth, i.e. hand filled with
my sperm, furtively wiping off on the white wall

of my apartment, later someone will sniff and say,
Oh, my, Kevin’s been a busy boy today

Me finishing what I’m doing, sending it
to Paolo Javier

I didn’t even know him when I wrote this,
I was mad to think he cared

Heavy Handed

When two people sit down to eat, after a long period
in which they saw each other in San Diego and
misunderstood the others' intentions, like me and Jennifer
they raise their glasses and say, "À la croûte!"

Let's eat! À la prochaine we will quarrel no more,
À la vôtre, I say, to her under the dark San Diego moon
on the balcony where the final scenes of
Jurassic Park, Part III were laid, or *The Iliad.*

How'd I get so fly there? À ballon d'essai,
a mere wave of a whimsical fan, try it, Chum, for once
you go Braque you never go back . . .

When two people are feeling heavy-handed and yet,
their hearts are like pink crystal pills, radically
transparent, well, ça ne fait rien—
never mind the bollocks, here's Kylie Minogue

all Gallic and Bardot-inspired since her very first date
with Olivier Martinez, cela va sans dire, or does
that go without saying? C'est bonnet blanc et
blanc bonnet, ça ne fait rien, he's six inches
of man or man inches of six . . .

My mind pacing on Wellbutrin, like a cat burglar
avoiding the chimneys of the roof, Paris skyline,
that's my mind, racing,

but always coming back to you—you thinking I was
lying to you, when I wasn't,

This one time I wasn't, when
I was heavy handed-
ly telling the what's the word? the truth to you
as we sat down to eat tasteless, lowfat nuts

Fly

All Greece hates
the still eyes in the Australian face,
the luster as of ecstasy tablets
where she wraps
a microphone around her legs.

All Greece begs
Kylie Minogue to lay her eggs,
a bird in a golden nest
which you could lay like a trowel
recalling Allen Ginsberg's *Howl*
—modernist screed, or coffee dregs?

Greece sees her fly,
to the prime minister next
to Michael Hutchence, in excess
the beauty of his cool feet
cramped in a noose
pushed out from tiled bathroom wall
the shower curtain thump,
white ash amid funeral *fragment*

Not silver, nor nemesis, nor orgone box
Shall cover thee,
Nor Dolce et Gabbana, nor many of
Allen Ginsberg's musical song poems on harmonium
or Nick Cave,
Nor the wild rose
nor last summer's wilder rave

Lethe has forgotten thee, and forgiven
your mother, who began this war
Even Iraq says, okay,
she had sex with Michael
Hutchence on an airplane, it's not
the end of the world, wrap it up,

yet Greece reviles
that five-foot pop princess and
the more I look the more I see
her story is that of *fragment*

Your Disco Needs You (Video)

for Matthew Greene

Hold on, Matt, gonna put you on the
manspeaker . . . *Uh-huh, uh-huh, "the flowers
that spring up from our carcasses will be
deadly?" Right on . . .*

Ever see that movie about the
last dude on Earth? Vincent Price,
or Charlton Heston, shivering behind
bolted door, then at sunrise, Will Smith,
he tip-toes out, watch further incursions
as zombie deer come lick at his cock
in empty street, repeat, repeat, I am the legend
Matt Greene . . .

At night they storm his shack, the
zombies of new Atlanta.

"One golden shot means another poor victim
has come to a glittering end."

Meanwhile massive trees have whispered thumbs
up to his painting

He paints so much his hand gets tired

Trees admire that about a man with

a golden gun

hopeless at Scrabble

sold on vanity

but that's so see-through

Ten thousand Kylies march in unison, mad
machine cyborg dolls, spelling out the
letters of her own name (and the word, "Disco")

She officiates at the massive funereal ceremony that marks
the death of the human, count backwards, 5, 4, 3, 2, 1

Hints that as everyone knows, "discovery" is a back
formation of "disco" plus the qualifier "very"

Ow fuck, I jerked off for ten hours in a row,
watching your paint dry

Oh my hand is a withered limb on the
tree of disco, vestigial and dry

Throw up the clay humans in a row,
one by one,
shoot them down in the carnival

Used to be able to split them to sand,
leaving the world to Goth armadillos, mesquite

Now, I'm not so sure. From Soho to Singapore,

"love is required whenever he's hired,
It comes just before the kill"

That Certain Something

I had an epiphany, Mama,
it was going to be awesome,
a trio of white, green and orange clouds
shaped like snakes kind of leapt up
into the top of the sky
spelling out my name
in the colors of Ireland or India
Was it real, Mama?
Or was it this Philip K. Dick illusion—that I
was *in love with him* but it wasn't really me?
Who had this epiphany
standing at the edge of the cornfield
with my ka-tet,
feet a-tingle, and Irish habitrails spelling my name
in letters that would soar one thousand feet high
—was it memories implanted in my brain
I wanted, once, years ago
but now I'd rip them out like Spike the chimp
that made him wince
rather than hurt another human being?
Tell me, Mama, that certain
something I felt like a rock in my chest

City Games

Released 17th or 24th November 2003 (UK/Europe/Australia) TBC
US release date TBC

1. SLOW
   [Kylie Minogue/Emilíana Torrini/Mr. Dan]
   Produced by Emilíana Torrini & Mr. Dan

2. CITY GAMES
   [Kylie Minogue/Richard Stannard/Julian Gallagher/Dave Morgan/Karen Poole]
   Produced by Richard 'Biff' Stannard & Julian Gallagher

3. YOU MAKE ME FEEL
   [Kylie Minogue/TommyD/Marius de Vries/Felix Howard]
   Produced by TommyD & Marius DeVries

4. E-Z ST
   [Pharrell Williams/Chad Hugo/Stevie Wonder]
   Produced by Pharrell Williams

5. IN THE DARK
   [Kylie Minogue/Emilíana Torrini/Dan Carey]
   Produced by Emilíana Torrini & Mr. Dan

6. HOW CAN YOU SAY NO?
   [Kylie Minogue/Dannii Minogue/Kurtis Mantronik]
   Produced by Kurtis Mantronik

7. SECOND THOUGHTS
   [TommyD/Marius de Vries]
   Produced by Tommy D & Marius DeVries

8. HEAVY HANDED
   [Kylie Minogue/Cathy Dennis/Kurtis Mantronik]
   Produced by Kurtis Mantronik

9. FLY
[Kylie Minogue/Kurtis Mantronik/Nickolas Ashford/
Valerie Simpson]
Produced by Kurtis Mantronik

10. ATTENTION SEEKER
[Kylie Minogue/Richard Stannard/Julian Gallagher/Dave Morgan]
Produced by Richard 'Biff' Stannard & Julian Gallagher

11. THAT CERTAIN SOMETHING
[Chris Braide]
Produced by Emilíana Torrini & Mr. Dan

12. BEAT U
[Kylie Minogue/Pharrell Williams]
Produced by Pharrell Williams.

I Know the Truth

"If, like a fairy godmother, I could give each of you one gift, I think, after long consideration I would choose TENACITY, because that is what has helped me most in those times of adversity that come even to the luckiest, like me."

—Margot Fonteyn, Durham University address, June 1990

I Know the Truth

I know the truth as lies in country clothes,
in poison, where our mouths stagger open,
snake's tongue in flicker on our chins.

What do you people want? The more you work,
the murkier the game plan. Down Tavistock Way
they're opening Pete's Better Plantains.

In deceitful love surrendered you
all the other truths I'd taught you in the movies.
After the timeout we'll lock down the hourglass.

Wind, sand, storm of stars, what is it you
demand of me, a child's bleak innocence?
I have gotten a rise out of you yet.
Tonight, natural forces, show me your shaolin.

Divine Invocation

To call upon a god
Happy he's happy
glad he will see me

Ringing his doorbell
Roses in wood frame
Ringing his doorbell

May God come out to
play in my sandbox,
climb on my nightstand

like toothbrush in glass
its pale water sad,
its tears whipped away?

I'm out in the back
Digging a hole to
the backside of Hell.

O goddess of love,
peel off the lyric
ring round my maypole

That woman in white
she looks quite a bit
like Kylie Minogue

Anagrams

Online guy, Neil Young
Canterbury Tales, rusty tabernacle
Marcel Proust, corrupt males
Kylie Minogue, I like 'em young
No real charm beneath Helena Bonham Carter
Michael Keaton, the coke animal
Julia Roberts, bestial juror
A really sublime twit, wait, I'm really subtle, William Butler Yeats
Revenge is our way, Sigourney Weaver
Erotica villainess, Alicia Silverstone
Andie McDowell, a wild old menace
No brains on a date, Antonio Banderas

Proverbs

After dinner is over, who cares about spoon? Deer
Should not toy with tiger. Every maybe has a wife
Called maybe-not. I went hunting for your proverbs,
Silently, dicta buzzing through my head,
In the long flat jungle where they stalk the plain.
If befriend donkey, expect to be kicked.

I missed the metaphor, my gun, like a loaded base,
stood up in my face. Impossible to miss someone
who will always be in heart. Mind, like parachute,
only function when open. "Hey, sahib," said my
Sumerian sidekick, "maybe in this one jungle case
you might be out of your league."

Mock insanity not always safe alibi. I didn't love you
because you were curious. I just let myself go, like
the mud turtle in pond, more safe than man on horseback.
I didn't give five dollars just to suck my dick,
must gather at leisure what may use in haste.
I'm trying to go all Charlie Chan on your ass,

Must turn up many stones to find hiding place
of snake. Okay, little clown, I suffuse this safari,
so bring me back to Minna Street, help me quit the crack.
I made a magic promise to pluck bullets from mid-air,
happiness from that hole in your rucksack.
Pretty girl, like lapdog, sometimes go mad.
People who ask riddle should know answer.

Ode to Walt Whitman

Half past ten, on Friday night on Harrison Street,
I saw the boys with the winter flowers
who pulled out of rolling ice cream carts their drugs of money,
Innumerable hairs on the back of his face
howled in the moonlight, summer and wolfman.

But none of us knew him, he was
totally a non-entity in the palace of the diamond.
I hardly took him to lunch before he had vomited liquid
a river of leaves on the white cloth
my lapels paraded in distant fountains.

Along the midnight eucalyptus grove,
that boy took a swim in the soft-scented airway
In the nostril of his cock
a tricky passage bought me a reservation
to the place where the buffalo roam, on
17th and Capp.

But who would wait,
no one really likes him,
no one but the people in the fern bar
for whom his piano playing is like Bobby Short,

when the stars jump down out of the sky, and
the night disturbs you, creeps under your
skin, the needles dancing from knee to knee
I knew you, you knew me, before you went to heaven.

San Francisco of microfiber
San Francisco where the Seals play,
what surprises fall out of your collar and cuffs?
With what little man are you dickering?
He is not far, he is only on Craigslist.

If I only had a brain, Walt Whitman,
I'd have waxed my dungeon to match your feeling,
nor your big waxy tail women laugh at,
halfway off like your Calvin Kleins
and your whistling shadow, menacing
the fellow travelers of US street fog

while you cried out my name,
my dick, my vital statistics, and how I came
enemy of Saturdays and Tuesdays
your twice a week vial
lost to you now in the aisles of Rolo.
Not for all the tea in your chin, vile scepter
that in sweating it out, you leaked from your go-cart,
dreamed of trying to meet Willie Mantle
in the green forest of your boyfriend swimming
the tiny ignorant pet you learned to mispronounce.

Not in looking back at your father, Adam Chandler from
All My Children, the beautiful son of Walt Whitman,
became like a moldy terrine
cluttered with old jars,
urine filling the bags of the school lunches,
I just couldn't stop moving long enough
to haul it out in Plaza revolving door,
it just didn't seem feasible, Walt Whitman

not just then! Not now! And look at him,
dust on your vacant sleeping nightstand,
blond as Brad Pitt, black as oh, Dave Chappelle,
lots of looks, just change your snakes and ladders
as you in your nose,
the fucked up fanboys, Walt, the partisans,
the fans of Kylie Minogue in mourning.

That one—Thom! That one—Alex! En pointe or
punctured only, they snore on your dreams
where Kylie is built up, a brigade of fat bladders,
with the tang of chlorine

and sunlight hot on her beach towel,
Matisse colors on my Harajuku boy.

How long did you hunt for those Oreo avocados,
or the jumper filled with rainbow nerf balls kids play in,
or the icy slick
where his stomach bulges from a cold cerveza
which Kylie's fans all rub in superstition,
as back we walk from the space station, on a pilgrimage of hope?

What you did built on nightmare, your pants at your ankles,
Tackle that would join the sea with the seaweed,
leather to your mercurochrome, fiery gym flower
and would subtract five inches from lover's TVotomy.

Since every man on the block's pressing nose to the window
in the white house glare of tomorrow morning,
up in the sky there's a diving board, flapping
and thwacking to mimic erection.

Begonia, begonia, suede, for men into emo,
this is the whirlwind, at this hour we reap it.
Down at the cable-car turnaround, skin turns to sugar,
US out of Iraq poses a question to his posse,
tiny flea bites reddening his ass, like some
crazy episode of *Inside the Actors Studio* with
James Lipton interviewing a penguin

What you can do, if all else fails, is bail
though vicarious sex is better than none
Tomorrow that pile of weaponry will emit a charge,
and minutes will turn into minarets in space.

That is why I'm wondering about your health, Walt Whitman,
I was the little boy under whose balls
you slipped your hand and coughed,
biting the pillow, wearing Barbie Solo in the Spotlight
in the velvety hush of dark,
and rising, took the bus to the men

retching twice before their dinner, little cubes of aqua;
not the men with David Gest hair,
not the men who lapped me in silence, like milk bars.
But you, against your self, the half-Pom half-Chihuahua,
tumescent shaft slick with light fluid,
lighthouse of Lodi, billowing harps of suede
to the tuxedo rental place on Powell by the bus stop.

Wondering how many guys you fucked wound
tight in hospital charity case, venom of margarine,
Wandering always
Fiercely in North America,
In pajamas in Havana,
Jocosely in Mexico,
In saran wrap in Cadiz
Ape over a Seville,
Cancer-raddled in Madrid,
On the floor in Alicante,
Delayed in Portugal—like a 747.

America can do that asinine Monday popcorn thing,
slaves of a boardroom, parish of troubadours,
flung open boldly to Special Edition Fever,
My heart is beating faster, but work is a disaster!
Ambushed by the timeclock on Adlai Stevenson's scrotum,
Let joy overlast him! Let Mordor mania
fire from your barrels
and Grey Poupon mustard tangle the shores.
No haya cuartel! Alerta!
A kind of sugar substitute for the high-strung
Let the rich, the hung, the fans of Michael Tilson Thomas
come to the back door of Symphony Glide.

And hello, hi, Walt Whitman, sleeping soundly with Rock Hudson,
with your long cruel hair wrapped right round his pole,
Blend clay with fog, in a tongue-proof San Francisco,
friends of the weather, Oprah-eyed charmers seeking a smelter.
Sleep, in your derma, sleep, colder than Edam,
Dance halls bang the pavement till dawn,

and American soldiers drown the desert nation Nintendo.
Let the unparalleled sweep of sanitation
renovate the flowers with the pale fur of your shiatsus,
let Lil Bow Wow, now grownup and known as Bow Wow, period,
bring a couple of ears of corn to Newcastle, plain.

Hymn

Turn around, bright eyes   the room, unfocussed   fuzzy

Sort of a churchlike feeling in this bar-b-que pit

pumped with flames

I'm sightless, the new age way of the blind, until

I turn around, bright eyes

Golden hair, the spaniel of Elizabeth Barrett Browning   dogs who ape

their owners' gaze   that flat button-like sheen of its eyes   nearly blinded

its neck swivels as she speaks to Robert Browning, in Italian

the dog understands, indeed he controls what comes out of her

tongue affair

It's gotten worse since you went away   Tariq Alvi

I was sort of OK, and then we walked across the Golden Gate Bridge

I'm afraid that, as a Muslim, you'll be shot wearing that phat jacket

It's only a line in the sand   I'm afraid to cross   and someday soon

a hot wind will blast my feet right through it

Hurry up, time, bring on the Oscars once again   inch worm

of the hours   slow, sluggish meatball, its yeast a-leak   Gold statue

I give to the first guy

who

invented the television set and the wheelchair

Travel in Light Years

Listen can you hear the distant calling? Carla approached me, saying, this
is going to be a shock but Philip has died
No, no, I wouldn't believe it. As Kylie said, "Maybe things that you
don't know are better."
Oh, she couldn't have been sweeter, but I was just shocked

By the power
Shocked by the power of love

But we have tickets to his show Sunday, I'm in denial and that is vinyl

Get up to get down at Discoteca

The little face goes round on DVD silver disk, as all alone
In the thundering noise of the plane, leaks the container

I'll take you in my capsule out of here

On TV people always eat Chinese takeout out of cartons
In real life we use plates, but it must be more pictorial for the film
Makers, those who say in charge, "Tight focus on container"

I think he was too alive to stay alive, it couldn't have been real

On Michael Brown's DVD we see him singing and dancing, mugging, the
World loves a clown, as even as Michael Jackson thrusts one
Knee into the camera's distance, during the closing number,
Man in the Mirror

You got to change   Yes, Rilke kept telling us all
During Modernism, and when I went away, turned my back for ten
Seconds, he, Philip, had slipped away
And all is changed sort of, still the drive to amuse and let
the questions come later, the sad beret

As though the world was too gray and he was in color

In some ways he was the benchmark for fun, and thus at the beach,
across
Pacific sands, confetti red and pink spells his name across galaxy

spell it "galaxie" for that is more the thing
and this urge to call back, to whistle back the little dog, that wet when
washed,
wriggles across Hayes Park on Fulton on diagonal paws
universal donor going
this way and that way
wishing that they weren't
going so far far away
into Thai temple of chopsticks
With not the single term limit of death
in terms of time, we're giving up light years
In the speck of paper from inside the compartment
he travels in light years
that read, *I'm shocked by the power,*
shocked by the power of love

for Philip Horvitz (1960-2005)

Action Kylie

Kylie Evidence

The pop singer Kylie Minogue was born in Melbourne in 1968 and started acting quite young (age 7 or 8) on such Australian-filmed TV series as *The Henderson Kids* and *Young Talent Time!* As a teenager her role as Charlene, the tomboy auto mechanic on the Australian soap *Neighbours*, brought her to national attention. "Charlene" was feisty, awkward, sweet; when she fell in love with "Scott," the boy next door, Kylie Minogue made the cover of *TIME* Australia arm in arm with Jason Donovan, the fresh-faced blond who played "Scott." In one episode Scott's "footy" team won a spirited match and Charlene grew so exhilarated at the party afterwards that she jumped onto the bar of the local and belted out the old Carole King 60s dance song "The Locomotion." Somehow this episode caught the eye of Stock/Aitken/Waterman (S/A/W), then London's pre-eminent pop writers and producers in the old Phil Spector mold. They brought Minogue to the UK and put her to work in their hit factory, recording dozens of unbearably catchy imitations of Madonna's great hits of the mid 1980s. The S/A/W brand name, attached to their giant publicity machine, made Kylie Minogue a recording star, and her first 15 singles all reached #1 on the UK charts. It's the same old story you've heard a gazillion times before. Pete Waterman also imported "Scott" (Jason Donovan), Kylie's offscreen boyfriend as well, and made him sing too, with pointedly less success. The two of them have a majestically awful duet, "Especially for You," which makes the Diana Ross-Lionel Richie "Endless Love" sound like Mahler in comparison. Most of these early hits are pretty crumby, but the best of them are pleasurable reminders of the permeability of image and the magnificent instability of the sign.

Every now and then I log on to perhaps the best of hundreds of Kylie websites, "Limbo," to follow excited threads such as "Who's More Enigmatic—Kylie or Jackie Onassis?" "What Kylie Has Taught Me," "Kylie's Speaking Voice," "How Tall is Kylie—really?" And yet to date I have only met maybe 50 Americans who know who she is, all of them gay men of a certain age and a certain artistic temperament, and only two people—the French photographic duo Pierre et Gilles—who have actually met and worked with her. It's almost as if she doesn't exist in America, and yet she's at the center of my universe. Well, that is the feeling, the *feeling of insecurity. When we're not together, tell me everything's gonna be all right . . .*

Wolfgang Tillmans's photo of Kylie shows her sweating in some loud club, a bottle of Carlsberg Lager propped in front of her, she's made up minimally, her hair pinned back behind her ears, she's all propped up listening wide-eyed to some unseen big man with a hairy fist and a giant gold ring who's gesturing towards her with stern authority. Or perhaps he's brushing her cheek with great tenderness. She seems alive—intensely so, but pale, like most of Tillmans's subjects, who all look so European and bubblelicious. She's only 5 feet 1, a toy, in a black T-shirt that's ridden up both arms. I'd like Tillmans to take my photo to see how "candid" his subjects really are but they seem like they are all so busy, too busy to notice his lens, oh well we're all on TV all the time nowadays anyhow, it's a fact of life like the climate or the white noise that surrounds us. All the light in the club is directed at her face and hands, which cup her chin, her fingers tapping at her temples. She doesn't look like a great brain. Whose arm is that, with its tattoo, its plastic beaded bracelet, and that gold nugget ring? Her face anointed with oil, the Turner Prize gleaming just outside the frame of the photo.square.club. The odd thing is that Kylie herself will never win any awards, for nothing.

In the book *Kylie Evidence*, a group of international photographers and conceptual artists play numerous variations on a single iconic image, the girl next door gone bad, the myth of Kylie Minogue. This hideous myth, so dear to my heart, is deployed in often ludicrous contexts. In the "Home of the Dew Drop Fairy," Karen Kilimnik replaces Kylie's image with a big red blowsy rose still life (to show decay), that's being stalked by a cunning little squirrel tasting the glassy dew (to show her innocence). Flip the page, there she is riding a carousel horse, in a sexed-up nun outfit, skirts hiked way up her thigh, in Pierre et Gilles's flashy, nutty hand-colored photo. Poor Kylie, detached from the artificial S/A/W soundscapes that made her once a beloved mascot for children, here assuming the suffering and fun of all the world. *I'll forgive, and forget, if you say you love me so, cos it's true, what they say: better the devil you know.*

Kylie was still dating Jason, and still under the thumb of her evil producers, who in turn were determined to keep their cash cow going as long as they could, when she met Michael Hutchence, the lead singer of Australia's biggest rock band, INXS. Instantly she changed from the girl next door to tabloid heroine. Asked what his hobby was, Hutchence is said to have replied, "Corrupting Kylie."—For he was the bad, Mick Jagger like Faust to Kylie's Marguerite. Everyone loves a good Harlequin romance, and this one was a pip. All of a sudden it was Jason who? Under Hutchence's spell, Kylie turned to drink, drugs, sex, art and bohemianism, and determined also to seize her own image away from her Svengali producers, finally finishing her contract and striking out on her own. Hutchence abandoned Kylie—the cad!—for the supermodel Helena Christensen, but our girl never looked back, and made a series of more sophisticated, "indie" pop records through which, bit by bit, she lost her core audience but gained a resolute and intransigent fan base of young gay male admirers. In search of artistic integrity, she attempted collaborations with a number of pre-eminent 90s rock musicians, including Prince, Lenny Kravitz, Bono, the Pet Shop Boys, Nick Cave, Robbie Williams and dozens more, and signed with a small, alternative dance label called "DeConstruction." Doesn't that name say it all? Alas, although she rocketed back to #1 on the UK charts with her first DeConstruction single, a slow, anthemic Revolver-esque ballad called "Confide in Me," subsequent releases failed to do well, and this period culminated in the debacle of her most ambitious LP, *Impossible Princess*, which had the misfortune of being released on the day Diana (Spencer) died, when British airwaves were ruled by Elton John's treacly Diana tribute "Candle in the Wind '98."

Of course Kylie had acting to turn to. During the PWL days she starred in her first film, *The Delinquents*, a 50s coming of age story—like *Splendor in the Grass* and just as dated. International films came next, but starring opposite Jean-Claude Van Damme in *Street Fighter* and opposite Pauly Shore in the ridiculous flop *Bio-Dome* didn't do much for her. She appeared onstage in the Bahamas in an experimental production of *The Tempest* (supposedly the actual setting Shakespeare had in mind!) but who is going to go to the Bahamas to see Kylie Minogue as Miranda? MAYBE Robert Wilson? Baz Luhrmann, the stylish Australian director, long a Kylie fan, cast her in his musical film *Moulin Rouge*, with Nicole Kidman and Ewan McGregor, but its commercial possibilities seem limited, and Kylie's part lasts only forty-eight seconds (she's the Green Fairy on the label of an absinthe bottle, who comes to life, flirts briefly with McGregor, and sings an odd snatch from "The Sound of Music"). Nevertheless sheer willpower won out and last year, in June, Kylie scrapped her arty, nihilistic vision and launched a full-scale return to the pop music that made her famous in the first place, with a new single, a new label, a new album and loads of press, and the music world gasped as "Spinning Around" became #1, and succeeding singles have done well too. She was the featured star at the closing of the Sydney Olympics in October 2000. People love that, everyone loves a great comeback. *Light Years* is a marvelous LP, filled with a kitsch instantly recognizable and resonant of 60s, 70s, 80s and 90s pop music and vibrant back beats, quoting from everything under the sun, unmistakably the work of a second- or third-rate talent more precious than any number of big time geniuses. This year there's a new album, *Fever*, released this month, Kylie purring over a 1982 bassline nicked from old Kraftwerk and Giorgio Moroder productions, and a great chart war overseas between Kylie and the nuttily popular Victoria Beckham, formerly known as Posh Spice, that rivals the war for the Rings of Power. Still the US knows nothing of Kylie at all.

If you've read Irvine Welsh's story, "Where the Debris Meets the Sea" (from his collection *The Acid House*) you know that Kylie, Kim Basinger, Madonna and Victoria Principal are all sitting around a house in California regaling each other with their private erotic fantasies. Sam Taylor-Wood's video installation "Misfit" featured Kylie naked, miming the recorded voice of the very last (19th century) castrato. Do we look to her to find out what's she up to next, or who can talk her into what? Who talked her into the recent UK TV appearance duetting with Ricky Martin on "Livin' la Vida Loca"? She was great, but my goodness, Ricky Martin!

Kylie is continually compared with her alter ego, Madonna, a decade older and considerably more famous. Everything Madonna does, Kylie does too. (Madonna *already* duetted with Ricky.) Madonna and Kylie make an almost religious pair, a diptych of Darwinian selection poked through the tight gaze of funk culture. It's my fantasy of history, poetry, interspecies warfare—that's all. *Kylie Evidence* is awfully like Madonna's notorious *Sex* book of the "Erotica" period, except it's more varied, well, it has to be doesn't it? Madonna is often called the "Queen of Pop," while Kylie is the "Princess," perhaps a younger version without the woes and cares Madonna is always foregrounding in her public appearances. Kylie without genitals, or with the genitals of a little boy, as in Simon Henwood's Darger imitations—naked but for a necklace, tiny tackle and all, permitted only a kind of genital power and a spectral innocence. She's more vulnerable than Madonna, but seems more resilient because she's from Australia. Kylie knows the raw power of the flat, comic book image, and the internecine enmity between language and image. *Evidence* plays beautifully along the thin line that stretches between irony and "true feeling," how one is often the obverse of the other, the Möbius strip inside modernism's motor apparatus.

In Berkeley this spring, after a poetry reading, Ed Gilbert and I were speaking of Kylie in muted voices, and then John Ashbery, whose reading we had just attended, spoke up behind our backs. "Excuse me, but did I hear you talking about Kylie Minogue?"

"Yeah!" I said, bowing to the polymath Ashbery. "How much do you love her?"

He looked bemused but allowed that he had seen Kylie's appearance, playing herself, in the UK sitcom *The Vicar of Dibley.* I haven't seen this one myself but apparently the Vicar has rashly promised to get Elton John to open the village fete, and the day seems lost until Kylie is produced as some kind of acceptable substitute. I hand it to John Ashbery as always—I have to, I wouldn't be human otherwise.

Her name—*Kylie Minogue*—is an alphabet from which all meaning has been scooped out, denoting a powerful sovereignty. Rearrange the letters to spell "I like 'em young." More often than not, the icon is in peril, at the mercy of words. Huge, dysfunctional words knock her over on her side. We her fans are evenly split, some of us preferring the "indie Kylie" of "Confide in Me" and *Impossible Princess,* some of us rejoicing that she has returned to her pop roots with *Light Years*. In Australia she has become an advertising emblem for "Pepsi Cola"—very Stuart Davis, clean, cool and marvelously articulated. Words will always spell peril for our heroine, once dubbed the "Singing Budgie." Overdrawn characters hover and rumble, portents seen in an angry dream, suspended in an ominous foreground of pure space. In 1998 the Japanese DJ Towa Tei released a stuttering, techno-house composition called "G.B.I." that features Kylie's vocals as disembodied chirps. "Hello / My name is German Bold Italic / I am a typeface / Which you have never heard before / Which you have never seen before / I can compliment you well / Especially in red / Extremely in green / Maybe in blue blue blue." She penetrates into the heartless, cutting blitheness of the word. "You will like my sense of style / I fit like a glove—ooh! / Gut ja! / Gut ja!" Cumbersome as office machines on wheels, words—headlines, gossip, innuendo, the language of "hasbeenism"—form layers of occluded meaning, their signs sublimated to the function of marketing tools as they peek around her tiny head in luscious bouquets of sick color. Black and white look best on her, but Minogue is a canny colorist and her use of grays, reds and blues is never wrong. Because she is so plastic, she looks different in every video, every photograph, it took me several months to be able to identify her from day to day.

But what does one do with one's enthusiasms? Where do they keep? There's an anxiety in declaring oneself a Kylie fan—similar to how coming out used to feel. (Nowadays it's the same exact thing I suppose.) Dennis Cooper can say, "Oh, I'm influenced by Bresson," and people will nod with approbation, even if they're thinking of *Cartier*-Bresson. I suffered some credibility loss while under the spell of Dario Argento, but nothing like the waves of shame and misery that engulf me when people say, "Kylie who? That girl who did 'The Locomotion'?" I think I like her because she reminds me of myself, I don't have Dennis's genius, not to mention Bresson's, but like Kylie I can stretch out a second or third rate talent and make it mean something by a) insisting on its smallness b) attempting to push the envelope, usually by collaboration with others and c) feeling no guilt when, in a corner, at the end of my tether, or upset by something in my personal life, I retreat to my roots and produce version XYZ of the thing I know you'll like from me. Do you think

Kylie's work is all about *post Colonialism*? That *Tempest* production sure was. "Kylie" is said to be the Maori word for "boomerang." This is often noted approvingly, as a boomerang "comes back" as often as Kylie has, but is it at all plausible? Queens appreciate the pathos of the Kylie legend, its cheesiness itself enormously appealing, the way Kylie survived a precocious stardom as "Charlene" to have sex with Michael Hutchence, who's not all that well known *himself*, and then to not even be the girl he hung himself because of. There's no Dennis Rodman in Kylie's back room; of course there were Prince and Lenny Kravitz. I flip through picture after picture, poke them out across the rug: an obsessive rendering, a trip-hop world of displacement and deracination good to go. Kylie Minogue isn't the first artist to find beauty in Freud's "uncanny," nor the first to locate the *unheimlich* squarely in the detritus of today's commercial culture. A purposive, kitschy flatness of gaze underlines her determination, the steadiness of her eye. What emerges is touching, almost saintly. Her critics say her voice sounds as though she's reading all her words off a prompter, that she lacks heart. Often she sounds as though English were not her own language. Kylie fans re-settle the unsettling haunt of sexuality by our insistence on customization—adapting, subverting its broad strokes to our own homey use. It's this impulse—gears shifting downward from public to private—that Kylie understands and illuminates beautifully. She extends this generosity to her own art, which seems unfinished, left to complete by the viewer. Thus there's an empty, spooky sigh at the heart of this work.

Iconic objects take on eerie lives of their own and no one knows their business, not even the moguls at Skywalker Ranch who control everything else. I can spot a fellow fan of Kylie's halfway around the room. We share a "secret understanding" akin to E.M. Forster's concept of homosexuality as a willed gift. Cold hard tears seep from this work, tears shed for an implacable universe of wanting and wishing and denial.

The Tongue Twisters

in honor of Kylie Minogue

The sixth sick sheik's sixth sheep's sick, as though the angry gods of the desert made me this infatuated with morgana
Where are all our oars? The crew boy's straining to touch his toes on He Boat
Brush each pretzel with a soupçon of ocean salt from the River Cam, then chomp down hard with
a wet red work rag
through which swift rivers rush.

Free flea spray they were advertising in the Cambridge paper the day I let E.M. Forster die, in a bed of
English horseradish sauce.
At Crooked Creek Camp the tired oarsman made a lap of my tent, I gave him the cockstand, asking with pretzels
how are our hors d'oeuvres?
Harsh censorship in UK and US papers and both houses of Parliament but after all it is only a boyish piss thing
that I wrote in honor of Kylie Minogue

Flowers and Money

Flowers and money I give to you,
these I hand you, because it's May.

We won't be happy having our
way, not this way, not this the

way of the fool, though so often
simple folly makes me feel I'm the

"guest" on a game show; and you're the
host. Tinny squeaky music plays as we

enter. "Well Alex," I whisper, "I
was in love for a week but all that's

over now." Pretty to say so, thus
appropriate, I thought, for

Spring anyhow. My accent fell
like a cut flower, like a crinkled

dollar bill, from some giddy
height into the gutter, a

"trashy" place for something
lovely or greenish. What a way to

describe one's own accent. I say
so who shouldn't, I give you money

and flowers, because I'm so happy and
because I want to—buy your

friendship, I want to be pretty
and appropriate, I want to have fallen.

You know like on TV the host gives
the guest a gift. In real life

it's like my mother always said,
"Don't go into someone's house with

empty arms."

Confide

after me, "I won't behave, I won't behave
till I cut off your nave," repeat after me in
the room with all the cold cuts

Good morning! To all the little children, like
eyelets, in rows, out my red front door in rows
who bow slightly, severely as I pass with my teacher

repeat after me, "I won't behave, understanding
should be shared," and then some kinkajou armed to the
teeth whirls in on visible threads, cuts the heads

of the flowers you spent all last year spending on
I could have been buying dishes. You bending over with
wet trowel, cool air on the seat of your pants

I'm trying to make you a shelter from your altar
one hand jammed down the front till the afore-
mentioned kinkajou kamikaze made us both sit up

and blink! One minute, peaceful kids or flowers, next
minute, crazed Australian rodent cuts through our yard
like boomerang nine inches above the pavement and

whammo. Confide in me you meant to do me harm
in those threadbare cutoffs. It's now or unthinkable, hit
or miss. Choice is yours. Stick, or twist? What's

mine is yours. Out popped the flashlight, sudden
blaze in the algae of me knowing you, wanting you,
endless puzzle in sixteen squares, one blank.

Then you keep fingering around the pieces till
you go mad, I go mad, kinkajou's jaws move rapidly
on stamens and pistils, heads roll and tiger troll

sits jauntily on rear window of slow moving Rolls.
We've all been hurt by love and we all
have our cross to bear. Then I hear you repeat

Put Yourself in My Place

Small circle coming around
steady, lamp light, crazy town
Where the rents go up
and we spin around

Please take a moment to
review our claim
I still love you and I
still feel the same

Mama when I wanted you
you crawled into toothpaste tube
like impasto on palette
of Picasso, you boob

And Daddy if your arms were
tired you dropped me
into the vanilla wafers of
madness on Madison Avenue

I hate the pair of view
in silent scream when ever I
think of your scarlet lips and
blue green eyes

Is it a family thing when
I took over your grim face
when I put myself in my place
on the Thursday race

Spinning Around

Move out of my way
A sharp reverential hustler

goes round the room
in the old-fashioned channel of "Quadrophenic"

on the couch under the window, head thrown back
in the New York sunlight

gray, even in sun, and out of the blue
did you ever have a mystical experience

He had me from "hello,"
not to take him for what he is worth
As, spinning around,
we patrol earth and the setting sun
mid-morning, and I'm wondering
does he know I'm alive

I know you're feeling me cos you like it like this
On days like this your
cock swells to proportions of egret
sleepy bird under my wing
As wise owl trembling, feebly, you stroke in the sun
Happiness that never lasts
Darkness comes to kick your ass
Long tall chicken when you're
seventeen I know you're
feeling me cos you like it like this disaffected queen

Yes I did have that experience
And wow, I am still not chilled out
I am giving you my mmmm,
                                        mainstream

G-House Project

LOTS OF Labradors
IN THE MATZOH balls
on your PARAMOUR

LICKING OFF the dough
FROM OUR dobro
in the FENCED-OFF MEADOW

G-HOUSE project
HE'S SO INTROspective
FOAM IS ALL flecked

GIVE ME Theodore
HANGING BY THE balls
OFF MADAME's FRENCH door

DON'T START ME wishing
KNOWING YOUR transmission
GAS HOUSE kicking in

INNOCENCE OF upper case
ALWAYS WEARS SMILEY face
OR A CHILLY grimace

SPEAK TO ME IN shouts
GAIN ON roundabout
HE'S THE BOY I touted

NEXT BIG thing
THIS SORT OF ALLEN sing-song
UGH MEYER LEMON juice

LOST MY TROPIC accent
IN A VEIL OF "Heavensent"
DOMESTIC DISTURBANCE

THERE'S ME AND THERE'S YOU
FORGETTING rendezvous
WITH A SWEDE OR two

IN ETHNICATED paradise
G-HOUSE PROJECT LETS slide
BLACK eyes on SLIM

Where Has the Love Gone?

written in honor of Brian Pera and Kylie Minogue

For all that I'm feeling kind of—*fragile*
Or *blue*, like my sash, woven in
Rotterdam when I was Dutch doll

Binging and purging on holiday sweets in
Rotterdam—when I was your holiday girl
If I remember correctly
Anyway I'm right as rain now, but where did the love go?
Nobody seems to know in any of the cages, I just hear these words passed back and forth, through the bars:

"Pssstt—where has the love gone?"
Even the card round my neck, tied with human hair, seems to whisper of a
Rapture once known, now evanescent
A love that couldn't exist when I spoke and talked about you, and I did you, baby

The Cats

They said they would never put any photos of cats in Artforum

The Cat

Try to catch the cat in mid-air as it
Jumps from the highest shelf in the room.

Ha, ha, there is no stopping me!

Cat's Cradle

Give me your hands, let's make a steeple,
tumble your fingers over mine

With the maximum number of fingers
I strike you out, your flawless gestures dumb

Yarn yawns from my fingertips to yours—
you have successfully aped the cat.

Cat Scratch Fever

When the lovers wake,
their naked arms yet throb with blood;
in the night Stanley was upon them,
marking them with telltale signs.

Hurry to the white, blue and pink tin in the
        bathroom,
Johnson & Johnson may hide away
the central fact of your love,
and that a black cat sat on your mat.

The Cat Dragged In

Such a lie.
Somewhere there must have been a cat that brought a human something.
And it was pretty foul from the sound of it.
Such a lie,
I have had two cats who gave nothing,
brought nothing, just waited, stood intent until
I turned myself inside out to see
into their eyes, pale and aglow,
then their little knees buckled and they
sat on my chest, a question and its answer.

Kitten with a Whip

On the same theme, Ann-
Margret traps the older,
married, horny guy John Forsythe

into making a pass at the
babysitter. In her yellow shell
angora, she's the kitten with a whip.

Her delicate little tail curls
underneath his balls,
feels good in a way.

Will he see me as a woman,
or am I only a thing in his
mortal kaleidoscope?

A man lives and dies, a
kitten's got this Ann-Margret
thing about youth.

Kitten on the Keys

I was so tired of the Rosses' cat
I opened piano bench, stuck the
howling cat into it

With all that sheet music,
there was just enough room
for one hideous calico with spots.

Piano music that all of it said,
Let me out at once or I
will never know anything but black

Cat People

Cat people in a quiet town
where you pay your bus fare,
and the screech of its air brakes jostles the air
Where fog reveals a face like a cat

At the gym, in the locker room,
You hurry out of your baggy, oversized trunks.
On the pebbled floor, they're humped with sweat
Is a cat in them, at the bottom of that silk?

Every other man on the street has that nature,
that at bottom his mother spent time in a tree.
Every woman on the elevator knows
down by her ankles whiskers poke a question.

In a quiet town in the 1940s with
refugees from Paris and wherever it was
Simone Simon might have hailed from, let the
doctor persecute, let my memories clear

Atavistic need bleeds from my paws,
I see red when I see a ring, even on my own left hand
Under the Val Lewton moon
there's a war on, or a loose-fitting blindfold,
for the firing squad that we whisper in rhythm

The Proverbial Cats and Dogs

Oh, that silly rain! Coming down on your head, so that
when you walk in my door, dripping, there they are,
on your shoulders clinging, like bridegrooms,
the proverbial cats and dogs.

Cat Scan

What's a cat scan, anyway?
You lie on your back, flimsy gown of paper,
and a cat walks down your body,
your forehead, your throat, sternum, stomach
and so forth, til the tiptoeing creature stares
back at you over his shoulder.
Kevin, plan to die.

T.S. Eliot

There was murder in the flowers,
piles of pesos wet with winter rain,
and the tall towers of Babylon
dressed in widow's weeds, dotted Swiss
cut-outs of cats appliqued just so.

Looking at them slouched in the armchair
I feel yet again
that those cats have pulled a number on me.

They don't howl or like that.
They're posing as skeptics
and the boys I once loved
come to me in a dream diner, like ketchup,
like chicken fried steak.

On the steam table, two cats dressed
in Maurice Sendak white aprons,
clang knives and pots in the night kitchen.
They saw murder in the flour,
eggs in the pain,
US intervention
in the desert heat, where cats are regularly shaven

I had been a hog
I had been hazed and shaven
I told them to piss on my leg and I came down the block,
pants open, a cat clinging to my secret.

I had done the thing you wanted
and what you did was fire me

Poor thing, you have the
luck of the cat
You won't make it back from Iraq.
That will be the final port of call
for a hazard,
is my guess.

I'm not dressing,
I'm lying down with the shades down.

From time to time I hear them singing,
outside the window

one of those songs
like Billie Holiday

or Lou Christie
“Sarah Jane, if my car could only talk to me
it would tell me ’bout you, baby.”

The Cat’s Meow

He wasn’t all black, and she
wasn’t all white

But when they walked together
in stripe formation, abreast

like a fish
zigzagging through the rooms of the apartment

And then when he left us
she walked alone, one animal

I would pull time down
off the highest shelf

I couldn’t catch it in my fingers
but on the carpet

like a spill of salt or sand,
it would twinkle. Bye.

The Magic Roundabout

American Idol

If we've learned one thing from this competition
it's that *song selection is key*
If Nikki McKibbin becomes our American Idol
We will have lost, she's raised the bar

I'm here with Ryan Seacrest and Brian Dunkleman in the
red room, where the boys and girls
Lounge around a red sofa with sleek red walls the color of blood

You're up next buddy
out of the mouth of a cannon, and if they asked me my prayer
it's to have my deaf parents hear me sing

But no one thinks to ask, have to drag it up myself
like a one-man frogman raising the bar
from the Titanic from icy ocean floor

Fish bobbing by, their big bulbous eyes near blind
We're forty thousand feet below the level
which once, we didn't even think about, we just were there

Living ordinary lives, me in San Francisco
grabbing the phone, you in Vancouver shelving a book,
Bob and Chris reconciling, Dodie's mother

in Hammond, the long ward of chemo patients
visiting and playing cards, Casey in his first day
of journalism school at Berkeley, we were just there

Vince Fecteau's sculpture pieces all molded together
he spits on them to seal them, then throws a few
twigs and seeds, bright tiny finery filched by a magpie

on McAllister Street, Bob Giard boards the bus in
Milwaukee and never makes it to Chicago,
his bravura prints frozen forever, in Durham

Thom Main slides his hands down his thighs
exposing his mole, upstate Hudson Valley
Joan can't think of what blouse to wear

finally remembers John Cage advice,
picks one out at random, my
cousin, Sarah Jones, on the cover of *Bitch*
magazine, twelve people at once,

a different world from the one those dead
eyed fish inhabit, I'd like to slap Justin Guarini's
mop of *Godspell* curls off the top of head

Give them to Randy

and now we're back to *American Idol*
as now way below the ocean slowly drops the jewel
the heart of the jewel, big gaudy sapphire necklace

Fish eye curiously, not even thinking
how deep it is here and the Titanic bar, lost its gleam
corroded by salt, the decks of the ship flash backwards

to a time when there weren't twenty-five
minutes of commercials to thirty-five minutes
of "show," when Stanley meowed for

our answering machine some treat in his
powerful *Jaws*-like jaws, his black fur
rippling with concentration and then

I can feel him in my lap, he was my
big boy, had nine lives, green eyes shining
when he'd had some broccoli

Oh my dear, he was only a cat
but oh! How we loved him, and how afterwards
the breath left his body as

the gods they roll the dice
their minds as cold as ice
and someone way down here
loses someone dear

An Audience with Kylie Minogue

for Justin Chin

The candy hearts, each one no
bigger than a nail, spill out on formica:
"Love Me," "Text Me," "Class Act," "E-Mail"
Wow, they have changed since
in the days when I loved you
"Got Love?" says this one, hot yellow dot
on a table of faint gray. Here's "Amore,"
something ethnic as I doll myself up
Heart in my throat, all itchy and fevered for my
audience with Kylie. Thinking quick
—like two triggers on two guns on each finger of the hands of Kali—
John Woo double bill baby! —Thinking like history
screwed in lightning I grab a few hearts
"Be Mine" and "Candy Girl" and thrust them into my
open palms, like blinky stigmatas. Then I pat
at the screen and the doctors pull back the linen
curtain. "My Boo." "First Kiss." "Dear One."
Hello, I cry out, *is anyone here? My heart*

is beating faster and work is a disaster

nothing changed since the day

in which I turned against you and my

little thing got hard and rammed back at me

shotgun

Blind

lovely pale summer dusk
driving to the city on 101, then lost, only a reading sign to stop me
I took you to an intimate restaurant

thinking this will be the first book I steal from the sand
pale yellow sand on Jellicoe
Island in the erect-o-cycle of Aran

It will be a fine time they are having I do think
when the curtain parts
sea on the left, and emerges

Victory Splashing
to an intimate restaurant
let me hear your body talk, your body tall-Kam-In-On
in the 19th Dynasty
his face glorious whiskey brown and

slide a pane of glass over his face
to prevent composition

it is not that you have not listened closely to Kylie Minogue
but you have been blind to pale, lovely
summer dusk driving to San Francisco or Boston
and Howard Carter is coming with steam shovel
crew of native laborers
On Glory's Course, stuffing it down my pants like a cold water bottle

Fourteen years old and
in country, dandelion head whiskery over
green clover of North Shore, Long Island,
pants pulled down to knees
and blowing away, blowing away

Bury Me Deep in Love

The traveler's face

Stepped on

Piccolo sound

Look, I see him through the ice

He's like, almost saying, walk on my face

Nearby the chapel
where

pinions flap in crystal breeze and dangling Christ swings from the cross

Should make a little fence round that face

Anyone got about seventy of those sticks from popsicles

I could make a little fence round the traveler's face,

bury him deep in love.

I know he's feeling this tremendous longing

Disturb not his rest yet invite him in, under your skin

Flute and violins soar around each note of sympathy

I'm totally projecting

like the stalagmites of this cave we stumble in with our vats of coffee

and whoa, this guy with fur

is in this little ring of ice

eyes closed, as if sleeping, slightly wrinkled skin, but pink

Wish I had my camera

but it's buried deep where the memory of this person lay fallow, like

thought under glass

Could have benefitted from some stem-cell research

Never mind, he is now with the saints

And what a fur coat he had

on the icy precipice

did you get this from Starbucks, it's some kind of Swiss roast

On top of the tallest mountain,
coffee tastes so good

oh forget about those little sticks

it was stupid

—I'm sorry

Two Swedish People

Accident—or murder? Where had two steady, faithful, elderly Swedish people vanished to? What had happened that they had said, or left, no word before going, or sent none? Questions, whether verbal or mental, that had no answers. That held us in a mounting uneasiness.

Good Like That

Work is a disaster
Treacle drips from the cherry tree beyond my window pane
slow fumes of treacle

My little nephew in the Persian Gulf says
His heart is beating faster and
War is a disaster
Slick in a white uniform, his head shaved, the top of his head a
  white ball

Oh! Noelle Bush, work is a disaster, I needed that Xanax
just to get me through the day of new job for internet
start-up, I called my own number saying, I am doctor Kevin Killian

Please give me white tablet in Lucky Nineteen, my uniform
as the nightmare begins in nation, starts up sharp DVD click
I'm listening, glistening, late for the disaster

And driving to prescription
My mom will have conniptions
I'm good like that
I can speak for US Navy, and my boys will come and save me
Sans souci, but I need to get my mouth round that Xanax
it helps me with my panics
It's good like that
The news is like a hairline
receding on the airline

And trucking to the Walgreens in my Wasp machine
Brother nations, picture this one of you tackled onto a point on
North Korea, and then way over here, a melted ice cream cone
in desert heat, another point, the axis of evil, then way
over there point three on the axis of evil

Hi, it's me—Noelle Bush, and that is my prescription I called in on the phone machine with my number of love from doctor Kevin what the fuck is his name now???

Hi! I'm the Green Fairy

whose face and body painted on poster of absinthe come to life when you've drunk enough absinthe
who shimmers in absolution taking the town on my knees in the air
the way Tim McVeigh, executed today in Indiana, contains my form in electric chair under lethal injection
I'm the Green Fairy for a gay mayor in Berlin, comrades and it's a good thing
who flutters in sparks of electrical new modernism, the birth of the cool in green Maximus poetics, rubbed up with Rem Koolhaas
whose red lips dabble the word of Oscar Hammerstein II, the only man plain from angelic plains of Connecticut
who caught the sinner by his toe
who put up the fleet wire to capture telegraphy, what I say goes, that is, my voice travels before me and after me, a cape of yellow stars that are poles through the green light of absinthe bath
who standing atop ladder of vertical wood slats takes a tumble on two toes and yet, because of flight, I hurt me not

I should know more about James Schuyler
after all this time on my back
Hi! News with a cheerful wee whiskbroom before I stumble myself into death, now pictured as a light bulb flickering out, say the second you pull the chain and pop
Hi, I'm the Green Fairy fresh from the pastures of Milton, Spenser and Marion Zimmer Bradley, stale yellow books held up in Muni to the commuters' faces, hanging their heads and clutching the glow tubes of Dr Pretorius
I should have seen it coming, like a train round the bend,
instead one beat before the end pop
Squiggle away like the scales before your eyes in the serpent territory of big time government *rifles d'arugula*
which hurt me not to dissolve your sleep into short bursts of excellent slumber of the dim, flood with asbestos, I won't feel a thi—

after Baz Luhrmann & Amy Gerstler

The Magic Roundabout

In summer 500

years back, in time, we hiked to the camera obscura, at our fingertips
a steel

drum with pictures deep in it of the shimmering, shifting sea we live on
All over the world dive bombers are coming to get ya

See, Leech, how various our universe, sheep tart as pies, and
girl on magic carousel

Me and Dodie in that dark circular room, so dark you'd
bump into a stranger, the life of San Francisco pictured on our
hands, in my
palm a silver shield awash in 360 degrees

everything you wanted to know about Gene Wilder coming too
soon (one,
two, three, boom as he put it),
girl drags dog on lead down bayberry hedge-lined path in
midsummer 500 years ago, San
Francisco, portobello cut-outs on kebab sticks, flecked with wee
squares of
wet red pepper
Leonardo invented it; it was the Rambaldi invention of its day; and we
really got
fucked up good there.

Prospero showed the magic roundabout
Saying, how the painted ponies fly up and down
Like him, time's over eager has snapped my wand
It is a dry thing gnarled by salt water and hung on
gallery walls by Matthew Higgs

I'll never let you go, it will be my mestiny
merely a dot on the map of time where the roads
end in a Western, *Major Dundee*

The things I won't do amount to a hill of beans,
It's destiny with a "me" in it—front-loaded like a glove compartment—
and so
when I was 27 I spent the night in Greece and
the oracle told me, I will never abandon you,
it wouldn't be mestiny

have you heard the whisper
that through the marble hall Delphi announced to me?—
Major Dundee isn't that captivating

When a dog laughs
It is nothing like what you thought it would be.
It is nothing in the worst
            sense of the word, a drop
in temperature from high summer to the low.
The low of everything else speaks
on the dog's tongue. Bitch laughs, and we
go on the down low for the time being, in
some mid-period Auden soliloquy.
Speechless. Cut like
glass, the laugh is nothing
that you know before or shall know again.

Speaking you
it was my mestiny
Rolling in a trickle, ash bent to burn,
four free men sorted out on a free afternoon

And in the Village
fire papers cascade into the square

I was so taken with you my
dick forgot to behave

Four three men sat past you
"Will I lose my dignity?
Will I lose my hair?"

They, the guardians of Pook Hill, bewitched the lowering veal calf
Disguised as the voice
Too wit, too wow
You're the greatest dancer

The life exeunts from fate, what's left
is mcstiny,
that which the state holds back from exception

It gives the moral inspiracy a ladder might,
to a puddle that looks up, your heel in its crotch
from Flatland to the sudden curve
of your ass, dude
and the winter skies beyond
They, the Robin Goodfellows of Tompkins Square
inflected by the fees
of an ordering ATMocracy
can be generou$
from this nightmare

Hey, Kylie—
When you were in The Delinquents did it feel like
a play on words?

I'm stressing out worrying about
you coming down with cancer
and cancelling what looked, from the outside,

like a person satisfied,

in a play on words
I was stitching nine
while
kinsmen of mine
wore holes in the marble steps with their knees,
pilgrims to a Mecca of health trying

to will you to live and then,
somehow I forgot and it was oh yes, Kylie,
still sick   oops

like that ad where Kate Winslet sifts through mementos in
Camden Market, recites all the odd things that
happened to her in her films as though she'd really
lived through them, "By 19 I was penniless and
heartbroken. I almost drowned at 20 . . . Then I
had my memory erased at 28 . . ."

She pulls back and remembers
Her life
Her card
Hateful, how hateful

But you would do that

Magic roundabout slows up and speeds up
Funnel of catcalls

Dodie and I filmed for Canadian TV
on Yerba Buena carousel, a carnival of her and me

yammering about our
love together, twenty years of it

Funnel of time

Tunnel of Kate Moss

spinning to hillbilly music on the carillon
for Justine Pimlott
bong bong

Fennel and thyme
radiant help
for Kylie
bong bong

bong bong

gathering moss
off the side of the boat
bailing out with tambourines or
your hands
for Tim Atkins

Take Me with You

Under the streetlight in a pool of white light
and the fist
closes around the light the
way I tried to keep you from leaving

he he ha ha love
slips away like the Clinton administration
band polled in Dade County, a trio of
black boxes wadded fast with thin gold
ineluctable chains thingold, hmm, you know, from
The Hobbit?

We can leave them all behind except for, well,
you can change your party affiliation
but what great colossus decreed

anyhow there would be
50 per cent Democrats and 50 Republicans and
why is it the national security threat
presses on our door like a Valentine

Tried and tried to grab the shrinking light that
like the tenor of mercury, falls like water on the
corner of Minna and Eleventh while I'm out

there having a cigarette,
take me with you
While 70,000 Marines in Mojave desert at
Twentynine Palms perch an hour from Needles
take me with you

that's the numbers of our plantation
and they call it "Moulin Rouge"

In Memory of Gwen Araujo

Gwen Amber Rose Araujo (February 24, 1985 – October 4, 2002, née Edward Araujo, Jr.) was a transgendered teenager who died during or shortly after being attacked by multiple individuals. The events leading up to Araujo's death were the subject of a pair of criminal trials in which it was alleged that the attackers were angered by the discovery that Araujo — who, at the time, was living as female — was biologically male. In the most recent trial, two of the defendants were convicted of second-degree murder, but the jury concluded that no hate crime was committed. The circumstances of the case have caused it to become a rallying point for the LGBT community, and a number of underreported and controversial aspects about the case and about Gwen's murder remain points of contention.

—opening of Wikipedia entry

Fluffernutter

They talk about this fluffernutter
Marshmallow frosting between two cakes
Maine ingredient in whoopie pie treat

Circular swirl of white cream

I was an old man splayed on the girth of Pierce
Around happy sandwich
Families displaying marshmallow, deposing potatoes
Universal fluffernutter mischievous, underfunded

"You know the world can see us
In a way that's different from who we are?"

Ballad of the Little Boy Who Began to Identify as a Pop Girl

Did you ever hear of Gwen Araujo born

Eddie Junior, and how in this godforsaken East Bay town

jumping with joy

she looked into big bag of gender tied to her back

probing, pulled one out, tried it on, liked it

A happy child but growing up in Newark

the ark of the new that affectless bunch from school and Gwen,

named after Gwen Stefani no doubt, penetrating

gaze like an eagle but did you hear the mother, Sylvia

speaking to those biological girls

They met on the street just hopping down to play some

dominoes, how ironic, what, that sort of placid game for kids

and maybe old mobsters like Marlon Brando, aged?

OK, so the boys liked her well enough

the first time around then the party of October 3

I would never forget that one girl

who ran out and said, hey everyone, she's got a dick

nor forgive that girl

but who was it after all

who stabbed and killed her with shovels

a frying pan and a can of tomatoes

not girls but   boys

you know the world can see us

in a way that's different—than who we are

then just   bury her in Silver Fork

name of etiquette   the silver spoon

trope of privilege   the boys and their rope

knocked the wall down

who knocked the wall down with gashed skin skull

then just   well, somebody talked

didn't he

gender variant youth

angel risen up out of mist and a sort of Jennifer Lopez urban

style, wings of desire   and—this drive for *I'm real and*

Aflutter

Pray not to die on this Pisgah blossoming with violets.
Pray to live through.
If you catch a whiff of violets from the darkness of the shadow of man
it will be spring in the world,
it will be spring in the world of the living
—D.H. Lawrence, "Craving for Spring"

I know you like it like this, I know
you're feeling me, spectral
knowledge grips me like mummy case
in the tomb of Howard Carter, enraptured,
so that, pink ray peering through stone door,
cracked open a ray,
penetrates Pharaoh brain,
like the third eye some people hang on their foreheads
I know, I know, I know
William Burroughs, murmuring, I've heard of you,
gave me the cold shivers,
I know, I know, I know
Aishwarya Rai, said Julia Roberts, the most
beautiful woman in the world

with that thing on her forehead

I'm not the same
you know you like it like this

the gesture is, to pat jewel onto her forehead where
somehow it sticks

Magisterial stick light

Burroughs looks up at me like some kind of lichen
Later, Mark Ewert tells him,

My friend in San Francisco was your
biggest fan till you

he had that heroin chic

Till you shot him that Spanish moss glance
out from under your hoary eyebrows, tangled wire

And now he's like every other liberal
You killed your wife, you're such a

pariah
I know, I know, I know

I'm not the same

Passing behind Bill I caught a whiff of
violet spray, scented igloo
in the wake of the dead

Pray not to die on this Pisgah
blossoming with violets Lawrence cried out
lying there coughing up

blood on the plowboy

He, my first student in the row,
made of clocks
ticking in violet thunders
I would pray not to die
still craving for spring,
first student in the snow
tied up like tinsel with this
knowledge thing that seizes me up so

Later when sated, I played him two numbers
by Kylie Minogue
his eyelids tighter than Dodge engine,

asshole trembling like the new leaf sign
that hangs over Market Street
in the spring breeze and creaks

hear it

On the Third Day

All beauty must die,
so, with a rose in his hand, he knelt
put a rock in my fist

In about the 10th block of Mission Street,
where the wild roses grow,
swimming uptown where I could be like a man

He was somehow out of luck, in a truck, teaching at Cabrillo
doing hand stands
now he's uptown

On the second day a flower so scarlet and blue
fell out of my eyes while I looked at your shoes
Demure as a trinket, and similar to

those hot plates people keep on her desk
switch on the light when the man
really pounds that ass

And my trembling subsided after the earthquake
of 1989 kickoff to the Bay Area world series
and say it ain't so Joe

Was feeling it down to my holy roll
it wasn't a twinge
more he hit me, and it felt like a

a muttered word
if I show you the roses will you
smile

Put a rose in my teeth
I know you're feeling me cause you
like it like this

Can of tomatoes
frying pan slam
the wall caves in

I know, I know, I know
he knelt down and
"they called me the wild rose
but my name was Eliza Day"

Is It All Over My Face?
You Caught Me Love Dancing

Is It All Over My Face?

Spring 1978, clutching old
copy of *Gay Sunshine*, on verso
Allen Ginsberg's poem
I lay love on my knee

"I nurs'd love where he lay
I let love get away
I let love lie low . . ."
in Stony Brook, Long Island where once

Denise Levertov nearly expired of an illicit passion in
wartime

Spring, so difficult to keep Allen Ginsberg's rhythms out of my head,
the numb, dumb beat that he compared to the stroke of a cock, its
pulse when you're holding it up (or out?) in front of you. His affect
was strong, unruly, he was so used to getting what he wanted, indeed
maybe it's a Buddhist trait, their accent on humility some kind of

bizarre coverup for the emotional thing
he was away on business
Always the two tails of his beige trench coat disappearing into subway
   car doors
Is it all over my face, when I talk with you I feel myself grow red, your
   wispy beard and heavy smell of cigarette smoke,
With you I feel the obviosity of Ginsberg's doggerel verse grow into
   baton-like accent and stricture, like it is going to pound me to death.

Is it all over my face?
You've caught me love dancing

Everything returns again, everything comes back, the return of the
repressed, both the laughter and the rain

She is living somewhere far away
and I send her this poem to give her options
ask her in my lonely way,

Today the skies over our little park are grim, pink, streaked with black
and white like a cat

nothing can hold back the rain

I could see through the clouds to this place where
Arthur Russell brings his hand around my cock
cello wet with tears, and how he's gone

I told my friends he was not the boy for me

Was I surprised? Yeah
Was I surprised? No, not at all

Desiree, you know how it hurts me, he caught
me love dancing

Heeding the warnings of Allen Ginsberg, the American Buddhist poet who predicted that their love would lead to untold suffering, he and Arthur Russell lived apart from the day they were married.

His death from AIDS in April 1992 inspired some of my own most beautiful work. My own premature death in June 2004 marked a great loss to contemporary Buddhist art. "Where do I run to? Is it real?"

Fifteen stitches across my face,
one for every man that hurt me.
Fifteen apparitions I have seen—the worst, a coat upon a coathanger.
Players and painted stage took all my love,
and not those things that they were emblems of. Is it
all over? My face feels scarred,
my teeth stretched across Botox and bandages.

In the silhouette he casts
the window of a moving train
moving faces—temporary hook-up
he touched the other side of my face

red maple
pepperbush
cranberry

is it all over the Internet, series of short,
    sharp, abdominal pains, is it
    common lingua franca the
    way my soul seeks to engulf you

is it all over my face, the shame
    of belief, the way the ears of George
    Bush Jr sprout from his head,
    for he fears the angel

is it all over the world, red
    maples of Xanadu, cranberry, the simple
    gift of Long Island, almost the way
        Arthur Russell, Lou Harrison played on it
        Allen Ginsberg all noble
        Arthur Russell, Lou Harrison played on it
        till sunset, spring, 1978, and far
        away fingerprints for Kylie
        on cat-tails
        still finds a way to haunt me
        always and forever

Always and Forever

Help me drop the other shoe before it lights on someone small, insincere. The bottle stands forlorn, a sign of a friend who, once home, now travels on the Marshall Plan. I wanted to give poor man Pedro some change, but in my pockets a gaping hole and my chance to do good lost for now to a muted trumpeter's swan.

I gambled with love, and in its stead I found status anxiety. Tears will fall, it's better to have given yourself a dose of salts than to burn a lamp on a Duralog. Always and forever. Feels like Satan's having a divorce in my ass. Not so handsome as to turn my head to the truth. A lot of me in these lines—that's the Wellbutrin; you could turn me over from time to time when your iced tea turns tepid. Noisy neighbors partying across the alley, and birds squawking, awaken me to a song dissolved in the dawn.

Almost a Lover

Two kinds of language,
    one the sort in which we speak to each other—
        the other hops about, on both feet, leaking semen—

That anxious feeling of erection,
    explode raisin deferred,
    or does it run,
    and then he said *that's pre-cum*

I didn't even know,

    No wonder I'm such a closet case.

        Two kinds of knowledge,
    one where one speaks to one's self

you minimize your distinctions,
    the other where you leak semen,
      almost a lover—

Kylie Minogue, you must get
    a lot of this;
it has happened ancestrally,

thus to you

It has happened in the balcony

to a muted trumpeter's swan

        I fell in love with him
            who told me the name,
                made me feel convincible.

            It happened on a coverlet and
        oh, the stain of it.

There's a Dark Secret in Me . . .

Too late the last number came up on the screen for the fourth time and
the blonde says, "Work with me here,"
And God says, "Buy a lottery ticket."
Jokes that thrive on the Internet till poison puddles at my ankles,
sopping cuffs, turn them inside out, tiny fish of poison
We're coming to America from the 24th to the 6th and would like
If possible, a kind of tenderness from master

that doesn't exist . . .
Walk down 11th Street, feel the fever building up, the hunger for drugs
at expense of shoes on your feet, your toenails raw, ripped
"Got three dollars to spare," and it used to be a quarter
but then you lived in Ashland with some lesbians
peacefully accumulating credit
Now it's so different you barely feel the freeze
Lotto ticket stubs pile up like autumn leaves
except no autumn, I'm still sober
but I want the money
Most of all I want a focus for my attention besides Kylie Minogue and
I see all too well
how drug addiction could benefit me in
that one way
from back in the day

Jennifer Lopez parading through unfinished apartment complaining
I have to do everything myself and this space
is too small for the bathtub I have in my mind
Blonde streaks, soft focus
Stock, bonds, saffron,
Ficus, I wake up screaming Ashland peace so vivid now lost to me

Shingled rooftops of Prague, flood rising
All you see are the chimneys

Amber alert saves those two girls who
tried to kill their rapist

I'm high upon the tightrope and I've got
to get to you

In Southwest Africa witchcraft returns
people with AIDS turn on the witches
who must have exposed their condition
to the God, to unnatural

No stoning in the Koran

Story after story, if pictorial enough,
Competes for the imagination
I've been keeping my own counsel
in solitude, drinking a lot, thinking

Looks like the new Harry Potter
book will be delayed, I'm like, get a
ghost writer, don't disappoint the
little children of the world

> On the Kylie newsgroup our young Malaysian friends
> are smirking, "America Deserved This"
>
> for when Jimmy Carter visited Malaysia in 1999 they say
> he ordered the secret destruction of 9,000 Malaysian
>
> people who saw through him, a kind of
> tenderness from master that doesn't exist . . .

Human League 1982

Invited this guy over to small light room, dark wood on every wall,
  bumped his butt against book case crash
Romy Schneider died the same week so all around me wonderful
photos of Romy, insouciant, alive, young,
Out of memory never saw her
Filing all day
And I kept thinking, "What would Rosellen do?" slumped, crutches
  askew, on the porch in the snow while we were out having turkey
  distributing the gravy present of US thanksgiving
Surely she would bid me to live
to heavy electropop beats of Human League 1982
and sometime to remember she is not real
Books spilled on dimly polished oak floor
was not my fault, next day say, "He was a muscular son of a
bitch with a tan from Durango," little white filing clerk from
B of A already with this one skeezy mark high on right
ass cheek, and some
time to remember mechanical thud of beat, like a spasm of lust on the
  day Romy Schneider died—then a week later, come home, snow
and Rosellen Kern dying on front porch, Captain Kern's steely jaw
  surveying wreckage of Human League 1982
and for me, plague of GRID we called it just be-
ginning in America

Free

Free, the price tags shiny with white-out, it's free,
I go shopping with Dodie, the red shiny bag at Kate Spade
on Grant, let's go into Agnes B and see how much the
shirt cost that Chris and Brian bought me

Save, long time ago I thought you could save me
I pictured a dreamy little house like Elizabeth
Robinson's, with a sunken tub, but instead I settle
for Squalid Manor, Frank O'Hara's dull apartment

"Build thee more stately mansions, O my soul,"
I hear a voice that rings, it might be Kylie Minogue
the sexiest tomboy beanpole on the planet,
that which I walked in size eight shoes, for to

Buy the ones we saw in the window, May sun
splattering them with pixels, we saw our selves
the two of us, and I said, Ah, what's the matter with me,
I have nothing to look forward to

Ship of pearl, which, poets feign,
Sail the unshadowed main—
The venturous bark that flings, and suddenly
the pavement tears itself apart, a lift appears

Man comes up through the sidewalk
in front of Stella McCartney store in New York
a little bit down from Joe and Charlie's
To have seen so much, to have missed so much!

Why, next time we will do better, till our
bleeding feet spurt compassion in our hearts—
in our next life when, perhaps, we will return
as a shell on the beach and a little pink kitten,

Lucy.

TWEAKY VILLAGE

DEDICATED TO REBECCA SOLNIT

Abraham Lincoln

Story of Abraham

It was like some tremendous Leonard Cohen song from the sixties
That first you heard Nico singing,
Elongated drawl scratchy on vinyl, Story of Abraham.

Again you could not remember
What he had done to thrust your image
On the lonely mirror of his mind,

But he was Abraham. Naked. Hips wedged
Into a cane chair on Martinique, and he
Shattered the night with trumpets, Jim.

I was reading *Beautiful Losers*, my mind
A peacock feather doused with white liquid,
And the floor opened slowly, hello, my Satanic friend.

What did he do, this Abraham, that all night long
You who take after your mothers
Now speak his name in mournful whispers?

He is not cornpone, that would be his cornpone-ish friend,
That, fried on heroin mayonnaise mustache,
Spotted a drop on his nostrils, of your tonsils.

You were jiving, he was living,
And he knew you would not know
What he had done in the Bible, a blank page,

Fog of Abraham, in Nico's hot fandition.
She was tithing, you were writhing,
She will prompt you as she can.

Story of Lincoln

And what right have you to comment on my choosing to love the person I set my heart on? Merely because you and Ross have gone on record as stating that heterosexuality is not of interest to the human community? I was the law partner of the man you think so little of, and he, Lincoln, deserves the respect you would give to any other black-clad human of a species, be he gay or straight! And you in your high-toned two-color surrey of the month with the lampshade fringe bobbling at five miles an hour—you do not know what went down on those long prairie nights in the world's largest bed in the world's tiniest log cabin love nest in Springfield?

I used to say to him, "Lincoln, speak low, for the snows have ears," and he would josh me, reminding me my name was Speed and my mind was made of crystal, no two flakes the same, so I couldn't say whether Democrats crouched between the floorboards to let in their ears. I would see these little, fleshy excrescences like toadstools growing between the boards, or bumping up the broadloom rug, and to me I saw ears, the ears of thy henchmen. For Lincoln and I were free of ambition at night, other than a rage to know what an Illinois body tastes like with whiskey dripped on its increscences. However not you, nor Ross.

This was the debate in the House, if I had had a drop to drink in Springfield.

For thine was the mischief, and the slander, and the abuse of ancestral privilege! We were roommates, cabin-mates, nothing more, but in the 19th century we sailed an earthbound Pequod. And that night we were not divided. I had had but one notion of the years, from the time I woke on the prairie, unwanted spawn of widower Speed, the flat lands oppressing my mind, that someday I would see the mountains and the ends of the sea, and in the body of Lincoln I found me both Canaans. Pity you stooped with your pick-up ears, hearth crickets, to abysm me in your prison of shame! Be he gay or straight, he was my map of the territory, the copy that, in the years to come, would precede the original, so that now, to reproduce my state of mind, I cross my legs in Yoga position, balancing Lincoln penny on warm firm head of dick, he has not failed me and you simply lack the right to judge. Had you been in that bed you might not be so treason, so needy. You are a toothless son of man, and I, lawyer Speed, have felt wet snowflakes melt in my open furnace of rectum.

Tweaky Village

Five Years In

to a war that never ends,
I heard telephones, opera house, favorite melodies

US 30 million dollars an acre they say
of liberating a solid gold mine,
and the sold trinkets of the astor ray
Slither up from the eagle's nest, sold

Nemo, with your wet leather suit tugged,
I kiss you, I want you to walk
there are two great factors that you can see,

Underwater

All I See Featuring MIMS

The guy who boasted that's how hot he is

> I'm borrowing Alistair McCartney's concept of asshole printing for identifying boy criminals . . . "Once a boy is dead," he wrote, "the specificity of his asshole leaves the world"
>
> *—and all I see is you*
>
> In the passageway I squeezed past his enormous brim and into the porthole where he lay waiting, like a snake crawling from the left edge of the page to the right, then bounding back

They love the way the charm hangs from chop that compliments the ear that compliments the hand

so close down the shop

> When I was a boy neighbors won the supermarket sweep, down the wide aisles of Billy Blake's they poured big steaks, rump roasts, small dense items like cheese into the cart, cart after cart, more kids than sense

This was the acme of glamour, no wonder I'm fat, and my asshole

when printed looks like a smiley face

> The emoticon shop closed on my face
>
> Five years into a war without hands

Clock ticks on

That's how hot he is

Where he came to my door in a sweat, bare-chested, where he lingered fingering the glove box in the Dodge, where I said, this is where your 32-year-old ass hits the curb

Jonathan Williams: Gone Fishing

The folksy ways of my dog scraped his tail along the Oriental carpet. What ho, boys, I ain't been on the gravy long. Williams made a magnificent gift to me, a print of his 1953 photo of Jack Spicer in jeans and an Eisenhower jacket, standing on timber as though log rolling on the Erie Canal. It was in Fort Bragg somewhere, Mendocino County, and Spicer watched from the shore as John Allen Ryan, his clothes hanging off the side mirror of the truck, galloped into the twilight.

I Lost ME to METH

Keep seeing these posters of these hollow-eyed men
on the subway, on the door of the bus, on the billboards high
above the city streets, "I lost ME to METH,"

male, shaky, hand spelling it out
tragic clever

I was thinking of how I had lost myself to meth, which is
maybe what they meant?

                                        And all my friends, I moved in on this perilous lonesome
feeling,

But you aren't on meth, a little voice kissed in my ear,
You're fine, Mister,

If you have lost meth it is to age,
to the medications that make you smile,

That gaunt man on the sign,
(they all of them tinted in sepia, for when you lose your
self to meth you first lose your color), (you become a numb
gnome in this tweaky village of the Castro),

the rainbow flag all stripes of one sepia

and that is how I lost being gay

I tried explaining some of this to Raymond,
on the way home on the plane it hit me,

I lost me to THEM, THEM as a way of reading "Meth,"
It was in my head why this message seemed so rad

the paint the color of weak cocoa, and I lost me to them,
Raymond,

I have had this trouble since eleven, or fourteen,
scrambling to keep
up with this one ball, black and white, a soccer ball,
me falling behind it,
onto my face in the first dirt of the sixties

where you go I will follow

All others can go to ILostMetoMeth.com where probably paid doctors can explain it better, but I will be on ILostMetoThem.com, a destination few will reach the ordinary way unless you're really tweaking balls, your fingers hitting every hot spot on the keyboard, and wow, all of a sudden, you're on this site with dirt on your tongue.

It is sort of the Dannii Minogue of feelings.

A worthy girl turned into charity case,

And my resentment of that man whose cock seemed longer than he knew what to do with,

And that day in the market at Cannes when Sean Penn won the Palme d'Or,

Freaky satin ribbon pinned down his chest by three small couturières giggling, down to his white belt

It is your day to shine, Sean Penn, as seamstresses earn their keep by tugging at your ribbon,
spelling out the words of bread, "I lost me to Meth," exclusively on "ILostMetoMeth.com"

Skull with Jewels on It

In her new show Kylie comes down to the stage riding an elevated skull, huge skull confronting the audience with its own death, a skull glittering with thousands of light bulbs. She's perched on the top in red, singing "Like a Drug." We're baffled by what this means, how she could lounge on top of the skull's round dome and try to be sexy, when she has just emerged from a three year cancer battle. Is this her triumph over death? "Death be not proud," etc. Meanwhile the skull is grinning ear to ear, just like the $100 million dollar skull Damien Hirst displays on the cover of *Artforum*.

Skull with jewels in it, you have undone me again. I move my fingertips along my scalp, poking for the jewels in my head. When I am no longer here, save my skull and put it in a condensery.

Acronyms, for Derek McCormack

As ABBA reminds me forever and ever, you needn't have English to be absent.

I've known AWOL Canadians, Kurds, Norsemen, Iraqis—

almost a cabal of the indifferent,

sharing identical speck of mutant, rancid DNA, sir.

On a date, his ETA is, oops, sorry dude, I lost track of the time—

And at home, he's got the emotional range of HAL (from *2001*).

My advice, put him in your Jeep, put the fucking top down,

target the accelerator with your long-distance laser wand,

then drop his sorry self into the bonfire of the Legos.

With his tiresome obsession with the MILF,

you better deposit him, though not in my backyard.

You will find life more posh without his nasty little kink:

and no warrants outstanding under your radar.

Must I remind you of Roy G. Biv,

his scuba tank of painted insouciance,

who colored the rainbow with his heels of shazam,

one snafu after another on the road to Apollo?

Again, Bjorn and Benny had me sending up clouds of SOS,

till I managed to shoot the fool dead via swat team—

and the truth is, I should have handed him a tip,

a zip and a tip, dear, a tip and a zip.

Cannot Exist

Storm clouds in white sky, cannot exist
Was Hal David the best lyricist for Burt Bacharach, I think so, yes, even though every other song has the same theme, "without your love, I'd just die," a chilling sort of belly flop into death
You hear it once, it's strong, ten times, you get a little weary of that
Thanatopsis in a death-based culture
In Orono a sun melting prettiness ensured I cannot exist without dreaming of green men
Saying goodbye to Jackson Mac Low,
to Robert Creeley,
191 miles of Maine highway to exit 191
We heard how Philip Whalen, Lee Hickman, Joe Brainard lost their will to write or paint at a certain age when a certain mood hit them
Just stopped. Then years went by, then in retrospect the grave loomed back at them into life, you, Justin, walking alone amid scattered elms and then, with no segue, you're up to your ass in open grave, head-stone at above eye level, you're reading what they say about you, rest in peace, excuse my dust,
On the whole I'd rather be at Steve and Jennifer's house
        that's how hot he is

Repetition Island

Ten Years In

Five years in—
to a war that never ends,
I heard telephones, opera house, favorite melodies

US 30 million dollars an acre they say
of liberating a solid gold mine,
and the sold trinkets of the astor ray
Slither up from the eagle's nest, sold

"Five years in," what was I thinking?
It wasn't only the war, it was the collapse of the commons,
the greed of the moneyworld, my own laziness,
my shame, I was an addict, and I let lies continue to drown out my qualms, in favor of a bliss that contained and contextualized my own death.—Ethel Waters singing "Am I Blue?" in *On with the Show!* (1929). It was like going to a dinner, and on the menu, only one choice, you could eat shit, or from the other column you could order a slightly less repulsive make of shit.
Even activists must freak out sometimes about how little we've done.
But sometimes I think the only way out of the neoliberal globalism we're drowning in is a complete return to irony and Marxism, and both of them failed in the first place because they could not withstand the homosexual . . . Kylie Minogue, "Get Outta My Way" (2010), waving her hands at the wrists on the beat, scorn face, as if to say, fuck you, I'm off to another world that doesn't have your stupid scrotum in it. It wasn't only the war, it was action neglected, sectarian malice, a faith that did not allow for labor. So I fucked him.

that's how hot he is

All the Lovers

Outside the Disney Concert Hall,
Kylie has summoned a clutch of cold models in white underwear,

They clamber on white boxes pitching for the sky

Somehow she appears in a dream sequence,

Boys and girls kiss and poke and struggle for love

In California, where the major candidates for governor and senator
live the lavish lives of Roman emperors,

Carly Fiorina, like Nero, bought a violin
for everyone on her Christmas list, from Cremona,

her wood golden and thin as hair,

81 per cent of voters don't care how wealthy a
candidate is

You have to be rich to flourish

What came first, the wife beater or the social system
that allowed ever and ever more flourish

In the face of a liverish social despair
all the lovers who have gone before

they don't compare to you

Fetish Photography

Her waist is cinched, I hear that gastric whistle, in the intense blaze of black net,

I'm busting my buttons with pride.

All along the riverside, fetish photographers have set up their booths

With moistened tissues they dab their lips.

I was here in the Cold War dreaming of a cozier hole,

one in which big women, with tiny waists, could lean and loaf,

Why does everyone have to work all the time? (Do you ever ask yourself as much, Vladimir Ulyanov?)

Remember when Ginger Rogers said she did everything Fred did, but backwards and in high heels?

Makes Fred feel so small,

Like everything he went through to dance well she shot down with that high heels remark,

On national TV,

Telling his best friend he was a loser,

He sets his alarm, daylight savings time looms, when the ping happens in his ear, he leaps to his feet and in his head, his brain grinds down, he's thinking "You got to be backwards now,"

Takes a piss, backwards,

Brushes his teeth, backwards,

"Listen, I am alone at a crossroads,
I'm not at home in my own home,
And I've tried and tried to do everything your way,"

I put on my shoes backwards,
Watching you crawl into your corset, from the crown of your head to the prim perfection of your waist.

I took the letters of the alphabet off of the shelf for you,

Flinging them to the floor, the letters, Z, Y, X, W, was that good enough,

The words, the zebra, Y-fronts, X-rays, Waterford crystal, V-Day, U-boat, tea bags, I reeled them off backwards,

Then you said, a real man would reel them off backwards, words with a final letter of what I want!

Z first, Z last, the word is Pez

What ends with Y? How about boy.

What ends in X, the sex you'll never have.

And so on: yellow, Chicken Kiev, milieu, that, soul kiss, suitor, Iraq, bus stop, bastinado, interpellation, atom, Bill . . .

Okay okay, finally you succumb, I'm standing here with my pants on sort of, still half asleep, but I'm dreaming of a future wage,

It will be the day that you go down on me,

The day I get up to Austria,

Viennese waltzes lighting our steps, gaslight built into the dancefloor, women with feathery hats,

"Lovers often hum this soft and sweet refrain even after love and laughter cease to reign. They recall a time when love was unrestrained. With the dawn the night is gone but love remains."

Devotion

Years of agony knowing
from behind a screen of studio flack,
how much money Zito was pocketing, and how little

how insanely little he gave us back

Half a season of Tim acting dumb,

off his game,

yet somewhere in there a new *beard energy* puffed itself afloat,

like the inside of a lotus or artichoke

unfolding, unmasking, until by Atlanta, well,

What happened, boys?

—you know what Mays said, 1961,

"I don't compare 'em, I just catch 'em."

Punctuation

You perceive the zoo,

In a flurry of white cotton,

Emma Flaherty of white cotton, her hand to her brow at land's end

thinking, sure and it's a long time since I been over—

She is lying, yes, no, there *have* been four stops,

whistle stops of a train gone to hell,

two marks of movement, hag! Xplosive laugh scalds the wet pipe stops,

That the sound of the ocean tunnel breaking?

Too late we interpellate its need, its need to speak from inside the balloon.

Tweaky helium squeak.

Break down, tunnel of love, bury yourself in the graveyard of the Quakers.

You have looked at the zoo and the four animals

shift from paw to paw, tails curling around your barbell.

Repetition Island

Monday. On Repetition Island plant life is scarce, so the owners ferry in caterers three times daily, and the crew's craft table is piled high with the fruits of the sea—lobster, shrimp, crab. While his body is still fit enough for the screen, young protag Mardi is making as much porn as he can. "Drink more milk," scream his directors, since milk is commonly thought to render the ass whiter, creamier. Mardi leads a rigorous screen life, and naps during breaks. Someone has to do it. Someone's got to bend over and spread his own cheeks, after milk breakfast, after milk lunch, milk enema, before his milk dinner. "Hello," says the asshole. "Both of us were object."

The other day he was trying to remember what life was like before he landed on Repetition Island, but thinking that way makes a boy crazy. It would be a sign of weakness, of an inability to hold your milk. "Would somebody please stick something up my butt and shut me up?" he cries humorously. The sun breaks through the clouds, on the beaches pink gravel shifts continuously, obliterating footprints, drying out trails of semen.

Tuesday. On Repetition Island plant life is scarce, but the producers ferry in caterers three times daily, and the crew's craft table is piled high with the fruits of the sea—lobster, shrimp, crab. "I'm into white-fish," Mardi offers, knowing somehow that this makes his listeners giggle: they are going to find a sexual meaning because his voice is so light, his lips so red. "Drink more milk," scream his directors, since milk is commonly thought to render the ass whiter, creamier. Today he is filming a sequence in which he is raped by a she-male partly dressed in the costume of a county guard. "Hello," says the asshole. "Both of us were object."

"Where are you from," whispers the she-male into his ear, as an enormous stiff organ pounds him onto the scratchy sheets of his cell bed. He doesn't reply. When he rises stiffly his chest and ribs are welted with flea-bites. Darn blanket. "Would somebody please stick something up my butt and shut me up?" he cries humorously. The sun breaks through the clouds, on the beaches pink gravel shifts continuously, obliterating footprints, drying trails of semen.

Wednesday. On Repetition Island plant life is scarce, so shade is currency, big stars get sturdy umbrellas and the rank and file like Mardi haul their canvas parasols from set to set. Breakfast is lobster, shrimp, crab. "Drink more milk," scream his directors, since milk is commonly thought to render the ass whiter, creamier. His dresser surveys his rear with churlish skepticism. "Yeah, you're a white boy, but I need snow color, not freckle color." "I hate fucking milk." Dresser slaps his butt, leaves handprint. "Are you up for a milk enema maybe?" Mardi hums the Kelis number they taught him for their musical episode. *My milkshake brings all the boys to the yard, better than yours.*

The other day he was trying to remember what life was like before he landed on Repetition Island, but thinking that way could make a boy crazy. It would be a sign of weakness, of an inability to hold your milk. "Would somebody please stick something up my butt and shut me up?" he cries humorously. The sun breaks through the clouds, on the beaches pink gravel shifts continuously, obliterating footprints, drying trails of milk.

Thursday. On Repetition Island plant life is scarce, but the crew's craft table is piled high with the fruits of the sea—lobster, shrimp, crab. Mardi chugs down a liter of milk as Mr. Guilfoyle looks on approvingly. Guilfoyle flips up Mardi's kilt in the back, inspects his merchandise. *I've had my eye on you this summer,* he says, or is Mardi imagining this part? Today his ass features in a sequence in which one hundred Scottish boys have been slain and heaped onto a ceremonial slab by Braveheart. "Hello," says the asshole. "Both of us were object."

Guilfoyle or one of them has his passport. When he came he knew some French and Spanish, but just as it builds up creaminess in the glutes, the milk diet's hell on language skills. In the afternoon his ass is built up into a planter in a greenhouse sequence in a porn noir. A leather daddy in leather trench coat parades up and down the orchids; Mardi and other flower boys watch his boots from upside down. The sun breaks through the clouds, on the beaches pink gravel shifts continuously, obliterating footprints, drying trails of semen.

Friday. The crew's craft table overflows with the fruits of the sea—lobster, shrimp, crab. Guilfoyle flips up Mardi's kilt in the back, inspects his merchandise, drawing a finger softened by mayonnaise up and down the boy's crack. Tall stars—and there are some tall performers on Repetition Island, though the majority are tiny twinks like Mardi—swear you can see from one end of the Island to the other, just popping up on your tiptoes. "What's it like being so big?" asks Mardi, trying to imagine. Tall star blinks, his cock swelling in Mardi's butt. "From loading dock on one end to lighthouse on the other, it's a company town, bro." Or did Mardi imagine this part? Dutifully, he submits to his milk enema at low tide, hands and knees in pebbled clear water. "Hello," says the asshole. "Both of us were object."

Guilfoyle or one of them has his passport. When he came he had some friends and spanking, but just as it builds up creaminess in the glutes, milk is hard on relationships. In the afternoon his ass is built up into a planter in a greenhouse sequence in *The Dick Slap.* It's too white, the director calls out, and best boys rub down his butt with taffy and peat moss. The sun breaks through the clouds, on the beaches pink gravel shifts continuously, obliterating footprints, drying trails of semen.

Trouble at the Pole

A black cat crosses the path of the earth,

while the Left pushes a flotilla of citizens under the ladder, the ladder propped against brick wall, Yvonne Rainer slouching on it

Black cat, ladder, next thing you know a mirror will shatter,

seven years bad luck of Obamanomics,

And that was the mirror in which a man could once see

not only the sky but his right to make a living,

raise a family of two kids.

Uh-oh, a border collapses, toss a pinch of salt over your shoulder,

the salt the ancient Romans mined from the Appian Way,

the salt we pressed into ancient earth to deprive our enemies of crops,

it was like a hydra growing heads the shape of Brussels sprouts,

liberally,

under the planet—it began I guess when Santa looked up from his sluggish nap—the sleep of neo-liberal generosity—

to find the elves had taken to the Pole, as in other cultures workers take to the streets,

And in their caps and breeches said elves did bite down the pole with white teeth,

Teeth sharpened from thousands of years making toys for us,

the sons of men under their women.

And he said, vigorous Santa Claus, *take it back, take all of it back.*

Norwegian Wood

At Eleanor Harwood Gallery   Dodie asked me

did I ever hear of   K O sex   Mike was nearby

Mike leaned in, well you take four Ambien

I knew it was going to be the sort of story I'd regret ever hearing

until I tried it for myself, what's Ambien

K O stands for knockout sex   the kind you have

when you want to have it, but you just can't face it

Straight men, Mike said, who want to be sodomized

but know they won't like it, they take four Ambien

and then call me in the morning

Hello, where was I last night   I once had a girl

or should I say   when people say   they are "having" sex

what are they implying about their status

well, we own this one thing from Norway

does that make you Liv Ullmann?

In the white coat of crystal she lowers a tube to your body

Women used to like her in the abstract

She got all into scientificness   and when you see her

your heartbeat plunges   a cold beat of lead

and then call me in the morning

Wow Wow Wow Wow

Giving You Up

He was the man who circumcised himself,
impatient for the knife, pulled up his gown

in long, dim, hospital hallway, blade in one hand,
with practiced hand slid up his cock, and zam

blood spattered on white hospital wall tile, over
magic graffiti, "Rex quondam, rexque futurus."

Now he has a smaller dick but more self-
satisfaction

Tightrope

I'm high up on a tightrope

> High up on the passage between the vowels, a rope that crawled like a snake from one edge of the page to the other, then bouncing back

>> Do they have this problem in Japanese or Hebrew, I keep wondering?

> In Japan or Israel are the poets into genre collapse, the way I keep my heart on the mattress like a tin can of nothing?

>> Are those putative poets novelists at heart? So easy to push a little at your poem and all of a sudden Alice Notley is checking her wordcount every few minutes

>> In France in that little room, the red, white and blue intertwined in ribbons

I'm high up on a tightrope and I've got to get to you

Kylie whispering this song and then deciding, to leave it off her album,

All her best songs saved as B-sides or just leaked onto the internet, where they live on as fan favorites, where a life of their own ennobles them, where when they creep into Duane Reade needing something mundane as Scotch tape, shoppers start to shriek in excited whispers, à la David Cronenberg's *Scanners*

Cornell Woolrich: The Bride Wore Black

The light of the city streaked off below him like the luminous spokes of a warped wheel. An indistinctly outlined, pearly moon seemed to drip down the sky like a clot of incandescent tapioca thrown up against the night by a cosmic comic. He lit the after-the-dance, while-waiting-for-her-to-come-back cigarette. He felt good, looking down at the town that had nearly had him licked once. "I'm all set now," he thought. "I'm young. I've got love. I've got a clear track. The rest is a cinch."

Cherry Bomb/Heath Ledger

Cherry, can you see me? You've got the way to
move me Cherry . . .

In the vicissitudes of not believing in God,
but I believe in Henry Miller,

author of *Tropic of Capricorn*. Yellow roses
open in the dark of the crystal vase, I'm spilling
my beans over in a website closed but to

subscribers
Fans split on "Cherry Bomb," which some declare the best
of all the X-era B-sides, which others jeer as "Euro-

vision hell," as for me, I'm undeclared, thinking mostly
that Heath seemed like a wild name, Dionysian,
the boy of the moors, all mad fire,

while "Ledger" was Apollonian, like St. Peter
counting up your sins in his ledger when you
knock on heaven's door. Ledger, that is one

motherfucking MBA sort of book, pages lined,
sums entered, by a man who stands. Entering sums
in his ledger, browbeaten, Bob Cratchit kind of guy,
the quiet desperation of the clerk.

You made me feel like I didn't need to go to work.

You had the hands of a clown grown calm.

Feed me up sight with your cherry bomb.

So that you would cast Heath Ledger in parts that exploited both sides of his personality—mouthing Shakespeare in high school drag in *10 Things I Hate About You*, as a smart ass modern boy thrust into medieval underwear in *A Knight's Tale*, the gay cowboy in *Brokeback Mountain*, that which he did was the work of Attis

When Ledger died the blood of Attis sank deep into earth,
poetry rose from his seed.

In the pink of his bones we saw a better world,
with weird flowers.

He tore off his balls to bring ritual to a universe deadened to sin,

Obama doing that video "Yes I Can," with a straight face,

And McCain damaged by torture, a hothead, threatening
sanctions.

So that around the world flashed that one AP photo of Heath Ledger and Dannii Minogue hugging that Australian boy with Down syndrome at some charity event, hearts all over them, while we argued that "Heath" was "health" without the "l," a consonant instantly supplied when his surname began, "Heath L," they called him, "heat hell."

Smell of a Book Jacket

Kim Novak, arrayed in the dusty turquoise-y pink costumes Novak wore in Hitchcock's *Vertigo.* Every day Scottie Ferguson, graying private eye essayed by James Stewart, tracks his prey to the Legion of Honor, where she spends hours gazing at this Spanish infanta from the time of El Greco. Old time kin of hers? Scottie jots a note in his pad. He's half mental following Madeleine everywhere, and not a trace of Judy.

Under her arm she clutches one Birkin bag and a book, bound in Spanish leather, its rich smell infecting its contents.

Can a book be physically altered, the way Tom Phillips erased his way through *A Humument* (1970), by merely binding it in leather, letting animal scents inhabit and manipulate words on a page? Scottie's beginning to think so. Like alphabet soup you could switch the noodle letters around, on the gruel's viscous floating surface. Outside Ernie's, the swank five-star restaurant Madeleine dines at nightly, Scottie steams up the glass and yearns for a touch of that book. Its scent is telling his dick where to go. He hasn't a clue otherwise, but even his initials spell out San Francisco—the city of names, sheltered bookful of gossip and incarnation. Madeleine might be descended from grand Spanish royalty of the Maja era of Spain. She is after all devoted to the Mission, and at the proto-Church on Dolores she tends her own grave is it? Scottie pretends to kneel behind her, but he's just adjusting his underwear under cover of the twilight. He's all like, *this is only a book erection so how can it possibly count my lady?*

He wonders maybe he should dip his hard-on in holy water, or belladonna, for a man when he dies doesn't want to wear the traces of his seed, or the rod that fetched it out of him like dowsing. He looks up, she seems to nod, paying an allusion to the boy from Spain who brought the book to her doubleness. That boy was the first page of Spain, and she turned him.

Wow Wow Wow Wow

New LP, new day for Kylie Minogue,
As strength resistant tests on gay clinics here in San Francisco turn into some Dr. Seuss test of prying men from their doors
Looks like a mighty virus eats his flesh, jumping first,
A Tasmanian devil, or Javier Bardem in *No Country for Old Men*, straight for his ass, to shred the flesh down to the bones,
ham timbales out of what was once the urgentest organ.
Read my lips, "I'm into you," the virus seems to wriggle
through plate glass, plates spun in the air, Kryptonite seal of lead on his cock,

Microscope's on, you creep into it, you like it

Get me into the shade

Claude Cahun

Is it "K-Hoon" or "K'un," second syllable so tight and small it's not even
really there? Claude Cahun, French surrealist, and her partner,

Marcel Moore (or something else)? Kylie had that song, "More, More, More,"

was she singing of these two artists from France? But bien sûr one thinks of Britney and her comeback song, "Gimme More."

The center of attention, Claude Cahun stands in full harlequin drag, big patchwork squares, under a blond bleach and a haircut so short, it's nothing but cowlick. The mirror acts as a clearing ground for the rest of her personality. Is she sneering or just being someone else?

"There is no first time around," so nothing is new, but theories of social subjectivity, alterity.

Who was it first made that construction, "If so and so had not existed, we would have had to invent her?"

I've got a vulgar mania for citation

the face is not the other but
the center of attention

The Pre-Poetic

CHARACTERS *(in order of appearance).*

FELIX, a Berkeley student
TARA, his sister, a trance medium
EVELYN, a family friend

[FELIX , EVELYN *and* TARA ONSTAGE *in the big room of a Berkeley house of the turn of the century "Arts & Crafts" period.*]

FELIX. It's trying as all get out, Tara, for first I have to get past the poetic to arrive at the pre-poetic, I compare it to genealogy in a condom.

TARA. Felix, hush, I'm trying to concentrate.

FELIX (*to* EVELYN). Tara's a trance medium as well as a transsexual. She looks at me as though she'd never seen a normal boy. Nor been one either.

EVELYN. Respect her, Felix, and you'll get more out of her that way. Just as you would a safe or cipher.

FELIX. I'll respect anyone who brings me news of the pre-poetic.

EVELYN. We must all join hands around the table and keep our voices low and dim, like the lighting in a Zalman King film. I feel a strange tingle when you put your hand in mine, it's an oyster oozing into a parking meter.

FELIX (*fretfully*). —Of which there are so many in Berkeley. And they used to call this the Freak Zone. I used to walk down Telegraph stuffing poppies into policemen's barrels.

TARA. Is there a "Felix" among us?

EVELYN. She's onto something. [*Eagerly.*] Yes, Tara, Felix is right here!

TARA. I speak in the voice of the late Rosa Luxemburg.

FELIX. And what happens to Tara while she is being taken over by spirits?

EVELYN. She becomes imploded from within. See her dissipating, like the Orientalist legends of the shrunken head! God, it's creepy. [*To* TARA.] Yes, Dr. Luxemburg, we see you now! [*To* FELIX.] She's wearing a shawl embroidered by Worth, or Wordsworth, I can't see the label because she's wearing it right-side-in.

FELIX. And what is this "Is there a Felix among us" nonsense anyhow? She's my sister and she knows my name as well as she knows her Russel Wright.

TARA. The spirits are moody tonight, sweet friends of Rosa. They sense some consternation in this overly paneled Berkeley room. The arts and crafts of another era war with our modern thrust for selfhood.

EVELYN. Tomorrow I'm going to drive a stake in the grave of Gustav Stickley.

FELIX (*to* EVELYN). But you're right—she doesn't look like Tara anymore. Her face has changed, it's brutal, big, coarse and sallow.

TARA. Climb up the staircase, Felix and Evelyn, then throw yourselves down it!

EVELYN (*urgently*). You heard her!

FELIX. I tried that already. I'm not going up there again.

TARA. The staircase of the poetic, to fall to the bottom you approach the "pre."

FELIX. Yesterday's answers to the problems of yore.

EVELYN. But Dr. Luxemburg, can't you send some ectoplasmic simulacra of ourselves to make that steep tumble down Staircase X? How could we possibly link our hands still and yet throw ourselves down the stairs—

FELIX. Gene Tierney did it, in *Leave Her to Heaven.*

TARA. It's regular.

EVELYN. Usually Rosa sends psychic doubles to actually perform the stunts. She knows I hate heights, even the second floor. I'm not as attached as you are, anyhow, to the idea of precluding the poetic.

FELIX (*gritting his teeth*). It's everything to me, yet she toys with my it boy. Tara always knew how to press my buttons. When she was my brother I had the hardest time protecting my boundaries. Now that she's a woman I find her even more *uberkrackenfleissunderhagen.* Yes, get some white spooks to the top step pronto, Tara dear! We're not our own servants, we're independent Berkeley loving people. Evelyn's a friend, not a threat! She and the pre-poetic are like this!

EVELYN. Felix, it is dangerous thus to talk back to the dead.

FELIX. I know, I know, I feel a cold emanation from your hand.

TARA. If there is a "Felix" among you, Evelyn died not half an hour ago, on her way to the séance. Her brave heart gave out before the pre-poetic.

FELIX. My God Evelyn, is this true?

EVELYN. He, the subject,
is black and white.
Even his clothes are like telephones.

TARA. She is speaking from beyond the grave.

FELIX. Evelyn, is this true, are you really dead?

EVELYN. I made the long hard jump to the pre-poetic half an hour ago, crossing the street to get to Small Press Distribution. A car came out of nowhere, or a tricycle with an ice box strapped in front that said, "Fruteria."

FELIX. They always *say* those "Fruteria" peddlers sell drugs out of their cabs.

TARA. She is exquisite even as she walks the earth and throws herself down the dark staircase toward the threshold of method.

EVELYN. Come, Felix, I'll show you . . . don't be frightened, now, my dear boy. Seasons don't fear the reaper; nor do the wind, the sun and the rain; we can be like they are . . .

FELIX (*taking* EVELYN*'s hand as though in a trance*). Your hand is warm, you wear not the funeral clothes of the grave.

EVELYN. No, I bought this top at Ross, it was marked down fifty per cent and then you could take off another thirty per cent at the register . . . Come, Berkeley fanboy, mount these steps with me.

[*They climb the staircase to a point halfway up, when* FELIX *shakes himself from out of his trance.*]

FELIX. Tara . . . I mean, Miss Luxemburg, is Evelyn planning to kill me?

TARA. It's "Doctor" Luxemburg. Young writer, think of death as a friend. Once at the threshold, you will look down at the *mere poetic* as a god laughs at the ant parade on a hill of beans.

FELIX. I can't, I can't, I never did see *The Replacement Killers* nor actually read a word of Levinas. I can't die yet, I'm still young.

TARA. The enemy, after all, is in our own country.

EVELYN. Felix dear, do I look any different, I'm not—all I am is . . .

magnified, that's all, a kernel of popcorn popped to bite size through the heat of the pre-poetic.

TARA. If there is a "Felix" among you, I have a message to one who waits on the stairs.

FELIX. Yes, I am Felix. [*Impatiently.*] Does a sex change operation affect one's ability to recognize one's own brother? Good grief, Tara, when you were Trevor, and you and I were fraternal twins, Mom and Dad bought us tons of Beanie Babies, and matching belts and holsters to play cowboys and cattle with. I was a gunslinger from the great north, and you were Trevor the Kid.

TARA. Should you be named Felix, it would be wise to ratchet up your courage, take a few more steps to the landing, then hurl yourself down to the carpet below, undergo most active mutations.

FELIX. Okay, now, Tara, obviously I'm having second thoughts. And Evelyn, you're nicely dressed, with all your pulses, but still, dead is dead, I don't want the broken neck that attends a fall.

TARA and EVELYN. We can be like they are . . .

FELIX. Respect my hesitation or the game's off!

EVELYN (*to* TARA). He's firm in indecision. He's halfway up or halfway down. Suddenly I don't feel persuasion's the answer. I tuck my hands into his pockets, feel the warmth there. The warm band of his waist.

FELIX. I take back my name, despite your constraints.

TARA. I send ghostly hands of ectoplasm that waver through the particle-filled air of the séance room to join your hands around the waist of that writer boy.

FELIX. This is like, oh what's that James Bond film . . .

EVELYN. *Octopussy*?

FELIX. Yes, with all the hands.

TARA and EVELYN. Like oysters into parking meters we embrace your waist.

[*Unwillingly* FELIX *is guided up the remaining steps of the darkened staircase, then flung down to the bottom of the steps. He lies sprawled on the carpet, his neck broken, attaining the pre-poetic in death.*]

TARA (*coming to*). Oh, I feel so weak. And chilly.

EVELYN. Me too. I wonder if there's any Echinacea.

TARA. Felix must really be out of it, look at the way he's lying, a figure in the carpet of post-colonial thought.

EVELYN. Like those old newsreels of Primo Levi.

TARA. He never really has dealt with my sex change thing. He liked having me as a brother, someone to pick on, because I was never bright, not the way he is. One summer he stuffed me into an inner tube and rolled me down Telegraph naked. Felix! You can get up now.

EVELYN. I think he enjoys having you as a sister too.

TARA. Tell that to someone who believes it. Someone unstable.

[*Pause.*]

[TARA *walks over to* FELIX*'s body, realizes that he's dead. She realizes the horror of the situation and begins to scream. Curtain falls.*]

Genital Emotion

Did she say "genital emotion,"
    Or the more logical, "angelic motion"?

The teletypes pound like jungle drums,
hell of commotion on the Kylie international network,
it almost sounded like "genital something,
genital emotion,"

Like Frank O'Hara I have behaved disgracefully,
thrown up on Erica Jong, fainted at readings,
confused two black poets with each other,
been accused of not being able to distinguish
black faces, tried to talk Dodie into
posing nude with me à la John and Yoko
for *Brains* magazine, made a pass at David
Johansen, —and Chris Johanson—and Hanson, —but I never actually
        spoke the words "genital emotion,"
it is the bourne from which no traveler returns,
there's a line here, separating sheep from goats, men from boys, pumas
        from cougars,
called genital emotion,
You know it if you got it,

It is the most embarrassing thing that could
happen, outside of death
Now wow wow wow wow

In Memory of George Kuchar

Go Naked in the World

TONY FRANCIOSA. I don't want to sit in your living room. I don't like your living room. It looks like it won't be there tomorrow. Everything you've got looks that way to me: very impermanent, as though you moved in twelve minutes ago and you could move out in half an hour and not leave a trace. Well, you left your traces on me all right. Why can't I get you out of my mind?

GINA LOLLOBRIGIDA. You need a girl maybe.

TONY FRANCIOSA. Oh, I've tried that, believe me.—That bothers you, doesn't it.

GINA LOLLOBRIGIDA. Why should it? I don't care about what you do.

TONY FRANCIOSA. Julie, you're a liar.

GINA LOLLOBRIGIDA. Go away.

TONY FRANCIOSA. No.

GINA LOLLOBRIGIDA. I said go away and don't come back. I don't need you and I don't want you. Why should you come drifting into my life out of nowhere and ruin it? You think every time the phone rings, my heart doesn't jump at it?

TONY FRANCIOSA. Maybe it's time you answered, Julie.

GINA LOLLOBRIGIDA. No. I don't want to be loved or be in love or have any trouble. That's what love is to me. Trouble. Leave me alone.

TONY FRANCIOSA. OK, OK, we won't talk about love. Never. Love is trouble. Down with love, Julie.

GINA LOLLOBRIGIDA. I could believe in love. I think—I think I believe in loving you.

TONY FRANCIOSA. Oh I hope so, Julie. Why?

GINA LOLLOBRIGIDA. I don't know. You make me feel like being honest, and honest women have lonely nights. I don't want to be honest. I want to live on a cloud, a big white cloud, with nothing to do but dangle my feet over the edge and fool myself that I'm completely happy for a change.

Dialogue by Ranald MacDougall

Bear Mountain Barbeque

Flash flood on Bear Mountain, and there

goes the barbeque . . . hot coals in heated steam

buns, mustard, relish, down the drain as rain

beats down the amaranths, and under our feet
pathway "A" quick shivers into brackish mud,

Everything's moving fast, and look at the ants,

They, who always attend the picnic of nudniks,
gaze amazed, gobsmacked, surfing the flow
of an unexpected late summer storm,

All six legs hanging ten

I could cry for my failed barbeque
I had been looking forward to it all summer,
cured my sausage,
painted white checks on red blanket,
combed my hair

Then Syd Barrett died and Arthur Lee,
and amazingly you decided,
I'm not going to Bear Mountain

I'm not going to work on Bard College farm no more.

Without you I soldiered on, tossing
Foreman grill into the trunk, popping my
marshmallows so they'd have pre-holes

Just in case you decided to relent and
come back and had your fork with you.

And then this. Apparition on a
wet, black what do you call it

Dear George,

Like a human Slinky, you stepped into the bookstore at Guerrero and 24th, in dark glasses, an attaché case, a trench coat, a derby. Playing an INS agent you took great pleasure in telling Carla Harryman (the owner of Small Press Traffic, in a demure white smock over a black and white dress) that the USA was fighting the war against illegal aliens by giving up on LA and environs, and moving the border higher—at the Bay Area in fact. All of the city was to be drained and turned into a canal that would protect real Americans from Mexican invaders. Carla didn't like that. She was shocked. "My store—a swamp?" she cried out, in great luscious horror close-up.

Time passed. In two of Kota's early videos we play the media, functioning as human barometers to test the emotional temperature of the story we report on. In *Video 97* an earthquake hits a miniature San Francisco, tiny helicopters bob up and down, I'm the man on the street, reporting on the spot, my mouth agape at the crazy tiny things I'm seeing. You're the anchorman safe in a studio keeping it suave. With the green screen we could have been anywhere. In *Gascoigne's Instant Fame* we're sportscasters with screwy British accents, worried about Gascoigne's instant fame.

Couldn't think of who I wanted to write the blurb for my book, my collected film writing, and when I thought of you, I saw the sky grow pink outside my window like a Renaissance altarpiece. "A zig-zagging joy ride," you wrote, "through forbidden zones of wonderment. More gut wrenching twists than Frisco's Lombard Street tourist thrill. A mental mélange of melodic memories stirred to perfection with pointed precision. The perfect elixir for an acid-tongued titan to toss in the face of the timid. Its sweetness will surprise you despite the sting to the senses."

After this came, dripping with the alliteration you patented, what, what could I give you in return? Flowers wouldn't do for George Kuchar. In a gift shop I saw a box of magnets, each one small as your thumbnail, each with a different old-time postcard view of a San Francisco landmark, Chinatown, cable car, North Beach, Golden Gate Bridge, the hills, the blue skies, the bay, Coit Tower, the works. Skylines that perished around the time of the NATO pact. I got another one to thank Deborah Remington. She died before it got to her New York apartment. Now you. I sent a third as a love spell, to induce Elijah Burgher to come west to meet me. I should tell him, just junk the goddam thing, save your life, reject the lover's gift. Ain't nothing but a monkey's paw.

We did a play, *Love Can Build a Bridge*, which opens the day after Donald Judd's death, when the family gathers around at the local Marfa saloon to hear the will read. West Texas calamities, and the Judds—Naomi, Wynonna, Ashley Judd. Judd Nelson the bad seed. Everyone's back. You played Donald Judd. We filmed you in Craig's kitchen, staring at the camera's eye, shouting out Donald Judd's last will and testament. In the play an evil lawyer re-mixes the video will so that you wind up giving everything up to somebody you hated. To mime the futzing of the video, you re-did all your lines as though speaking through a crowd of static and crackle, your mouth moving around every syllable slowly, or speedily, stuttering and skipping. What acting! Technically perfect. "I'm from the days before the computer," you said.

Travis Jeppesen was coming to California and asked to meet me and Dodie. Why sure, I said grandly, offering to broker introductions to any artist or writer he wanted to shake hands with. Only one really, he said, bashfully, George Kuchar. There had been some big retrospective of your work in Berlin, and he was in love. I think maybe I can fix that up for you, Travis, I said. It all worked out perfectly, or sort of, the one day he had free you moved around three or four things and we went to see you at a big house in the Castro with many A-Gay celebrities there. Then we drove out to the Cliff House, no, the Beach Chalet, and had seafood snacks and lemonade. You took pictures of him and me, he took pictures of you and me, I took all the other pictures we would ever need as the sun sank into the ocean.

You were limping in Berkeley and within days the feeling left your feet and ankles, your lower legs. Within days they had moved you into the hospice. You would never again return to 18th Street, but the world found you where you were. I loved the story about the elderly man who made a voyage of many miles to meet you at SFAI, and when you showed up he was nakedly horrified that you weren't George Cukor. "But he's dead," you said apologetically. As one of twins you had every right to think you were going to live forever, but that wasn't your way. We shared a crush on the 40s Fox star Lynn Bari, another on the rebellious underdog Sal Mineo. I gave you books about them. You gave me Lynn Bari in *The Amazing Mr. X* (1948). The day before your diagnosis, I mailed you the life of Tab Hunter, but you had gone before it came to your door. Time passed, luscious in great horror close-up. Should have sent the flowers instead of those goddamn magnets.

Autumn Leaves

JOAN CRAWFORD. Emotionally upset! Of course you want me to commit him! Get him out of your life, put him away permanently where he can never again remind either one of you of your horrible guilt! How you, and you, committed the ugliest of all possible sins, so ugly that it drove him into the state he is in.

LORNE GREENE. What kind of woman are you to be satisfied with only half a man?

VERA MILES. There must be something wrong with you.

JOAN CRAWFORD. Even when he doesn't know what he is doing, he's a saner man than you are. He's decent, and proud. Can you say the same for yourselves? Where's your decency? In what garbage dump, Mr. Hansen? And where's yours, you tramp?

VERA MILES. I don't have to listen to that.

LORNE GREENE. She's the one who's crazy.

VERA MILES. She'd have to be crazy to put up with that weakling.

JOAN CRAWFORD. You: his loving, doting fraud of a father. And you: you slut. You're both so consumed by evil—so rotten—your filthy souls are too evil for Hell itself.

Dialogue by Jean Rouverol,
Hugo Butler,
Lewis Meltzer,
Robert Blees

Same Time Last Year

Same Time Last Year

"Knock knock, anyone home?" I've come for my regular chalet appointment, for once a year we meet to rekindle an old romance. Empty salons. Corridors. Salons. Doors. Doors. Salons. Empty chairs, deep armchairs, thick carpets. Heavy hangings. Stairs, steps. Steps, one after the other. Glass objects, objects still intact, empty glasses. A glass that falls, three, two, one, zero. Glass partition, letters. One of them boasts a picture of my face on it, bobbing and bouncing on the soft European air conditioning, like a balloon. I'm so happy to see him. It's been exactly one year, but will he remember me?

My lungs are pure oxygen, my palms sweaty like the face of a robot. I better play some NIM first.

I need distraction, I've got fifty bucks riding on the chance he won't even recognize me. So what if he does? Fifty bucks riding, what does that mean? Does that mean I'll be out 50? Seems so cruel when I'm not exactly, you know, in any shape to throw around my money. "Knock knock," I repeat, weakly, to the Mozartian halls I find myself in, rows of men in tuxedo jackets and women dressed in slinky gowns and feather masks. Rooms with huge mirrors and high, high ceilings, everything made of cut paper like the origami Hiroshima victims cut into cranes.

In NIM, you remove several objects off a row of similar objects, and you make sure there's always at least one of what you're moving left in the row when you're done. Like shooting ducks. You don't want to literally shoot all of them and thereby extinguish the whole duck race! You need at least one male and one female to propagate themselves, start a new generation, eggs, ducklings, toddler ducks, teens, then drakes, and then you can go crazy all over again with your Mannheim. So leave you some dots on that line, line two also, line three for sure. And don't forget that the player who makes the first move invariably loses. It's built into the logarithms. Me—Parkinson's? No no! I'm just nervous, that's all, so I keep fidgeting with my NIMS. Spooky here in this ancient chalet in autumn.

Kate Bush, "Wuthering Heights"

Heathcliff—it's me, your Cathy, I'm coming home, it's so cold, let me into your window! I was only a boy when Kate Bush made that song a hit, and I fell in love with her gaudy, Lindsay Kemp "interpretative dance" skills. The way her long arms would wrap round her own ribcage, hugging herself as she zigzagged like a Pharaoh across a field of barley, poplars swaying behind her, her flame colored dress—or pantsuit—like a blazing provocation. Hugging herself, as though, like Heathcliff, she had been cast out of society for some unnamed offense related to her fabulousness. When she sang the words, "Let me in-a your window," she raised a pale hand and covered her face with it, then let the hand slide so that the face seemed to be approaching a window pane, pressing its nose into it, in mute appeal, longing for the warmth inside of family life. Yet forever cut off from it because of her red dress, her orangey-red dress like a flamingo. It's me, your Cathy! She would mispronounce her own name, placing a heavy accent on the second syllable of "Cathy," making it sound like "Ca-*thee,*" as if to say, I don't even care what I call myself, I'm beyond names, I am need.

In 1968 a French movie critic, René Prédal, published this list of possible, alternative "meanings" of *Marienbad*, with the approval of Resnais. I found this on the IMDB FAQ for *L'Année dernière à Marienbad.*

> 1) X comes from a parallel universe, where his version is "right," his attempts to get A away from the hotel are doomed to failure because he's not really "there" (only A and M are seeing him)
>
> 2) X is lying, and creating a fictional account of "last year" to seduce A (this is actually the explanation often cited by Robbe-Grillet)
>
> 3) X is actually A's therapist, trying to force a removed / blocked memory out of her. The whole setting is just a fantasy of A
>
> 4) X is Death, coming back for A after giving her one more year of life, but he cannot "steal" her until she remembers and

agrees to go (this is an ancient Breton legend—Resnais is quite fond of Breton folklore)

Nominated for four Academy Awards, Robert Mulligan's 1978 soap serial *Same Time, Next Year* used the Robbe-Grillet structure just as playfully. George and Doris, married to others, meet one evening in 1951 in a Northern California vacation resort, have dinner, wind up in bed, then panic the next day at the thought that they've been "cheating." At the end of the weekend, they go back to their spouses, but agree to meet every year on this date, for the rest of the lives, and to keep this ongoing adultery a secret. The film drops into their lives every five years, so we see them change not only in looks, and the simple matter of aging, but through the changes in US and world society of the same period. By film's end they are in their fifties—rough, grizzled veterans of 50s suburbia, 60s angst and 70s rage and liberation. Ellen Burstyn and Alan Alda play the pair through thick and thin. Obviously based on *Last Year at Marienbad,* the charm of the film is waiting to see how they're going to look the next time we see them, and Mulligan's costume and hair designers rarely disappoint.

5) A is dead and the "hotel" is really Hell or Limbo. M is some sort of devil, and X is trying to bring A back to the realm of the living

6) The whole set-up is the result of a failed time-travel experiment (a situation Resnais will explore in 1968's *Je t'aime, je t'aime*), and X, A and all the hotel's guests are caught in a time-loop, of whom only M is aware. They are condemned to relive this situation for all eternity

7) The *Morel's Invention* alternative—M has invented a machine that creates a completely believable virtual reality—except him and X, all the other characters are "fake." The machine is looping, and thus X is reliving all the same events again and again (it must be stressed that Resnais had not read *Morel's Invention* until well after he did *Marienbad*)

8) We're just seeing the rest of the "drama" acted in the hotel's theatre, A is just imagining herself in the role of the heroine out of boredom

Prelude to a Putdown

"She can be very seductive," have you ever heard this phrase without its corollary, the putdown, something like, "but she's utterly mad."

"I know she can be very seductive," by itself, is not really a sentence, as it lacks the requisite follow-up, "but you're making a huge mistake."

"He can be very seductive," I have heard it said, "but for God's sake, Gary Glitter, he's only 25."

As a prelude to a putdown, "she can be very seductive" has few peers. I have lived through decades of English and heard this one a million times. What type of person says these five words? People haunted by their own imaginations!

GEORGE. I know he can be very seductive—

DORIS. —But what, George? What? Take that hookah out of your mouth in the 60s and spit it out!

GEORGE. But he's from the streets—a guttersnipe—and he'll pull you down with him, Doris.

In *The Mail* on Sunday, one of Keith Urban's early girlfriends warned Nicole Kidman against hoping too much. "When he talks the talk, he can be very seductive, but I'm not sure Keith will ever be ready to settle down."

> 9) The "hotel" is an asylum, all the "guests" are insane, A is suffering from schizophrenia and X is just a figment of her imagination—M is her doctor
>
> 10) M is a scientist who has populated the hotel of living mannequins, X is being just the subject of a strange experiment
>
> 11) Nothing really strange is happening—the story is banally

the attempt of X to have A remember their affair of one year before (who she does remember, even if she's denying). All the "strangeness" is just a deliberate attempt to mislead the audience through clever editing

12) X has never met A, but he dreamed of her—he's genuinely convinced they had an affair "last year." All the shifting realities are just part of his defective memory

"Can you even tell me who we'll be driving with? That way I'd know what to expect."

"Do you always know what to expect in life?" he says without looking up again. "Maybe in America you do, but we are not all Americans, happily for the world."

"For me, this isn't a holiday."

Instructions for Kota

Gray strips,
smiles of gray,
cut them from the wall,
let men and women see through the wall,

Break out half a cup vermouth, one quarter cup mustard of
  Dusseldorf,
red potatoes, small like the eyeballs of lovers,
cut black strips black as movie telephones,
strips white as lace,
In the LP by the Monkees, it was easy then to tell weak from strong,
right from wrong, but today there is no day or night

Today there is no black and white?

GEORGE. —Why do you have to look so luminous? It'd make things so much easier if you woke up with puffy eyes and blotchy skin like everyone else.

DORIS. Guess God thought chubby thighs were enough.

GEORGE. And your silences! I have never heard anyone raise his voice in this hotel—no one. The servants are mute. Do you know what I heard, that last year at this season, it was so cold that the water in the ponds froze.

DORIS. What do you want of me?

GEORGE. But you always stayed at a certain distance, as if on the threshold, as if at the entrance to a place that was too dark, or strange . . .

DORIS. You are like a shadow—and you're waiting for me to come closer—Oh, let me alone . . . let me alone . . . let me alone!

GEORGE. You know what the worst part of this is?—While I'm thinking all of this, I have the most fantastic hard-on.

“What You Cannot See Is Truth”

Tales from a Spooky Gallery Floor

Will you stay the night at Barbara Gladstone gallery? All night, for reals? Nerves up to it? Feeling lucky, boy?

Like the *House on Haunted Hill*, I saw as a kid, an oversized skeleton swoops on wires from the theater rafters, its long dangling fingers grab at the hats of the moviegoers—

Whoever agrees to stay in the house all night long will earn ten thousand dollars each! The guests are trapped, with ghosts and terrors, and hors d'oeuvres—

—no electricity, no cell phones, no keys to the door. Blind, my feet stumble over body after body. Life's too short, I knew that! So why are all of these, my friends, dead or dying on the gallery floor?

Welcome to the house on Haunted Hill intones a voice profundo— from hidden speakers built inside the walls—

"Since it was built a century ago, seven people, including my brother, have been murdered in it, since then, I've owned the house. I only spent one night here and when they found me in the morning, I . . . I was almost dead."

Was it a nightmare we were collectively dreaming or mayhap the triumph of the Koch brothers, that turned our bodies into clay, our joints to wire, our cocks and cunts into jewels and berries?

Announce the death of the common space so that each place, each warehouse floor, each forest glade, is owned by the rich, its airspace, its gravespace, the space between, even the invisible world in which the magick used to happen?

I am his fourth wife—the first one disappeared—the other two died.

In the morning when you find me, kick my ribs in, make sure I've gone to my maker, not to no devil. Watch the last ectobreath of life flutter up towards the dark. Mister Ugo, keep those demons off of me, prithee!

Nude

I can see myself slumped against the wall,
my shirt tucked awkwardly—my socks up,
in some past era, the decade of the cold and desolate where-did-I-go,

Music streams from under the floorboards,
medleys of pop hits from big band era,

a heroic-er age than ours.

Mice and gnomes watch me anxiously, whisper,
what song are you listening to,

Oh hi!
"At last my love has come along."

For that song you should be nude or you should be
wearing a big white satin ballgown, lilacs pinned to your shoulder

or angry at the capitalist system for leaving you
near death, your joints akimbo,

on the dusty floor of house death-within-life

"At last my love has come along," —Lynn Bari sang it in *Orchestra Wives*
(1942) and at Obama's inauguration Beyoncé sang it while president
and first lady took tearful smiley first dance—
—at home, Etta James scowling, rocking, shouting out to the Lord,
"That's *my* song—*mine*—*mine*, you hear me?"

Violets in the Snow

Black wax on blue rare earth—
Blue trinitron from the Congo

Did that girl swallow a Santa hat?

No, she has fur on your teeth

And she be giving you
that Chloë Sevigny look

Sort of seductive,
but fragile—
like violets in the snow.

TV newsman holds up dirt, that sifts through his hand onto tin pan: "Those gray specks are rare earth minerals. I mean, they're nondescript. They're not sparkling and shiny like gold or diamonds or anything. But they're—they're just as important."

And Mubarak adds, "I plan to go."
back straight, arms folded, dogs squirming on the leash.

We fear the man behind the curtain—

Thing is, there ain't no curtain, it's us.

Link

I think we need to see some link between these eight bodies on the floor, a factual link, to make sense of the death drive,

Foolishly I posited that one had slept with another, then he with her, and so around the floor, a slow moving windmill of lust—lust and loss,

But it may not be that narrative.

What is that need to explain the nude? It comes from within, from spatial relations, or am I a novelist through and through,

as once I wanted to write for the soaps, *Santa Barbara*, *One Life to Live*.

The reason she's in that corner is that she wants to avoid that man's gaze, for she is the sister of the bride he left at the altar,

Cornell Woolrich reasons,

George Kuchar reasons.

What is your favorite link between the living and the dead (pick one)—

Ladder

Lantern

Séance

Telenovela

Scotch and Tab

Rose bouquet

Coins on the eyelids

The affordance is perfect, but from
time to time one must intervene in the conflict, step up, clap hands
sharply twice, clear your throat, say, “Boys no squabbling.”

The bodies are like something from Racine,

Ce n’est plus une ardeur dans mes veines cachée:
C’est Vénus tout entière à sa proie attachée.

"What You Cannot See Is Truth"

Sky a deep blue, an Umbrian blue, above the gold towers of San
Francisco . . .

Watching Argento's *Mother of Tears*, in which a haggard Asia plays
an art historian "and an archaeologist"—
blow dust off a bannered inscription
in some unexplored catacombs, and up pop words:

"What you see does not exist," she translates for our benefit.

What's that bit down there? "What you cannot see is truth." And over
the Pacific words fail to pierce the tongue,

In Bangkok Peter Christopherson lies dead,

uncrowned and broken, the sturdiest little alarm clock,

his lips move

his greatest enemy, the lie

Through dark catacomb he prowls, pausing for the merest moment at
the dizzying staircase,

Vertigo would freeze a lesser man,

"It is not the man who descends, it is the world that lifts up"

Sky fills with blue, more blue, blue filched from every corner of Earth,

I'm sorry for you for evidently you don't have blue where you live,

It is piled up above me, like the laugh of Saint Sleazy

Nude Valentine

Pick this gerbera daisy,
pull off its petals, one at a time,

don't freak out when they
don't come out right

"she loves me, she loves me not,"

The word "not" so harsh,
like a dogbite

Tempted to cheat on the daisy,
you can look ahead, see three "nots"
and three "yeas,"

then the flower, nude,
falls to the dirt,

I loved the luck of it,
I loved not the luck of it,

I loved it when you sucked my cock,

It was our slang for love,

you would pull my daisy from
out of my Levis,

I wanted to die then,
so happy,

your finger tapping my asshole,
happy valentines day

Link

In an art space—what is commons? What is communing?

The somatic practices of curriculum.

Reclamation of public spaces: concensus versus *decensus.*

The majority of the body is frontier.

As Tim Dlugos wrote, "The corpses change but the party goes on forever."

The body is biologically incomplete. What's missing? It's a simple question. Can a body be a commons? I hear that it's cold way down there, Laura Nyro sang. Crazy cold way down there.

Speak Right

Can you hear me? Nations led like Pygmalion at the promise of Galatea,

The need to make inert flesh come alive, behave like a girl—

the need plunges through mind to war.

Can you hear me? It is believed that, if one takes the right tone to this work,

speak directly into its heart, its animae catch fire, brachioles sway and merge, kingfishers catch fire

Frankenstein bends, his head bigger than the moon, sits up on the table,

Linen sheets slip away from his loins,

Body looks at me, quietly moves its mouth, "Hello living man."

Then you have all the chazzerai about, you created it, now you're responsible for it.

Udo Kier did this so well in *Flesh for Frankenstein*

the Baron coming to hate his creation, trying to find it a gay mate,

then, shrug, I ain't no pimp—speak low when you speak love,

speak into the monster's ear.

Hello bodies, I am here to visit you for one night only,

Tell me your dreams, as you lie across enchanted forest floor at Barbara Gladstone gallery,

the stone, the glad,

Were you my friends from former public life, did I kiss your mouth, were you thinking of my breath as you lost your last,

I was in your lap, digging and growling like my dog, finding the warm spot, come dead friends, you are almost alive,

the wax on the wood anoints you into Lazarus calm, you might push away the stone, announce your life naked,

Linen forgotten at your feet, your genitals bright and rosy,

Your eyes clear for once, I was in love with you from far away,

You seemed not to care then, I was in agony,

Did I wish you dead then? Or did I wish merely you had never come to life in the first place, to torment me with your cute haircut, and your grinning face so similar to that of screen star Joseph Gordon-Levitt,

Speak low as we fall adrift,

"You laugh when boys or women tell their dreams. / Is't not your trick?"

In this room give me your madness, bring me your youth in a jar, the snake on my breast that sucks the nurse asleep,

come give me your kind words, "hello living man," how once I jumped out of my seat, while driving, when my name came up on the screen

In the gallery with Scott when your photo rolled across the screen and the walls fell away

Nude there, white walls and I was thinking, is this what want is about,

you've got the gift—then out of poetry some words drop out, scattered like corn fallen from the cob, words drop out and those that remain, like teeth in a skull, lisp when they mean to sing,

Words fall down

It is a tree with blood stead of sap,

Speak into my ear, speak right, bid me to live.

Words drop out like futures in my 401K plan, I look for you, I scan the room, there's no "you" in it, there's a gap between gravestones,

Valentines

You have left for Brussels,

could have sworn I heard your whisper,

I am reading these signs that the infidel hates me.

TONY GREENE ERA

The Birth of Pallaksch

The Birth of Pallaksch

1.

Saw R.H. Quaytman speak last night, a luminous slide keynoted the screen, behind a tall podium she stood,

Her gaze rapt and quizzical, the screen a bonanza of pink dots and yellow coronals buzzing like bumblebees, but they do not move, they only seem to move . . .

Jack Spicer, "when the taxi does not move, it does not move."

"Op art," she said, "like humor, or sex, presses our yes and no buttons simultaneously."

A world of scotched humor,

A pileup of missed connections, on Craigslist, "It was I whose cock you sucked at the Ramrod, and though I put my card into the breast pocket of your soft white shirt, I know sometimes I send my shirts to the laundry but miss those pockets entirely . . ."

"When the taxi does not move, it does not move. Burn it as quick as you can."

Often the shirts come back with a wad of coiled paper sludge in their breast pockets, some stained with blue ink, some stained with pencil, gray flakes in a shifting line, like the coastline of California . . . I'm wondering if you slipped your card into my pocket and I was so enthralled I didn't hear you . . .

The shape of that slither . . .

There has been a rose down . . .

A mastication, a crunch of the jaw . . .

No mastodons but dawn,

In the ancient ray known to the ancestors as Sun Ra,

He came to Berkeley and taught in my classroom.

Sound, he said, is a form of travel. They wake you up with sounds instead of buckets of water because it's more economical.

It has that Pallaksch feeling in Berkeley, he said.

It has that perhaps and mishaps feeling, of yes I'm wearing it and no, I don't remember what I'm wearing.

I'm not owning it, as I might have in the 70s.

In 1971 in the fall, Sun Ra came and stayed, we read ancient texts and burned a taxicab, we had the Mishka bear carved into the hair on our groins, the little bear of the Berkeley people.

Into the lounge stumbled the boy with the bear dangling from one arm,

I'm Christopher Robin, it's perfectly true,

And I have the Pallaksch feeling for you.

My bear is my amulet, my hand is the spring,

I injured my hand on the rock for you, wet blood sprang from my wrist like a spray jet,

It was quite real,

Felt like it was burning.

Wait, I cried to the retreating ship, don't leave me behind in Croatoan, I'm the guy who built that sign,

You didn't even know how to spell it,

About words you had only the vaguest concept.

They are falling into a thicket,

Wet leaves on the face of a book, open to the sky.

2.

Father enfeebled,

Poking a hip out of the bed, he is easy to spot,

Weak father with varicose tray, the air here wan and twisty,

Not hungry, lost my appetite, ask him why he says,

I'd rather be in Philadelphia.

Last night in Clarksville he was leaving for the station,

His suitcase in his hand like a traveling man,

And now his life's a slouch

He was my father,

I guess that would be something, eh?

3.

Why has birth been deified? Through the time-lapse option on your Flip, you can watch a baby born, expelled, flying through the air and aging, again, till he or she dies, thrown into a grave.

If it is a poetic movement, then it is some baby.

The sort you wish would stay in their high chair, but no, here they come, tall and menacing, their baby clothes ripping apart with each step, as a baby hand rises patiently to tear off its constrictive bib.

Not for Baby Pallaksch the palindrome of "bib."

No palindromes, in fact, for they distort life, give a false picture, an image rotten as old teeth in a barrel. Those sneaky, hypocritical sons of bitches, the palindromes, with their fair and balanced look at what, at the word which reads the same backwards and forwards.

Tear off the bib, Pip, spit up the pap, Pop, shut down the radar, fuck Pop and Mom.

This movement has its own volition. Abandon old kayak, old racecar, old level at noon. Eva, can I stab bats in a cave?

No, Mel Gibson is a casino's big lemon.

4.

"About words you had only the vaguest concept.

They are falling into a thicket,

Wet leaves on the face of a book, open to the sky."

Yes, that was me huddling in luddite formation, in a cave, bare hips squatting on my heels,

building a fire out of human sinews,

wondering about life outside the cave, its great tall creatures

sometimes so graceful, sometimes flashing murder, tiny eyes,

Around my waist a string made of vines,

From the vines a pair of clips,

these hold my cock and balls on me. I'm pre-righted identity, from a fumbling savage to a, well, I'll call myself "man," prehistoric "man," and I'll have these genitals to show it.

Now attention is focused on the string,

And nothing will be allowed to fuck with it. These marks I'll leave a million years, and one day Werner Herzog will stumble on my leavings, and make a film of the birth

of the Pallaksch,

3-D,

In luminous French Lascaux, where I lay scalded, beat, my flesh flattened by air flies, my teeth in a grimace but my drawing still luminous, still a pre-vision

the rusty clips lie nearby, scattered in cave salt, as once,

in the 80s, Chris asked me and Dodie, for a young poet what is the easiest way to get into *Sulfur*?

And she said, write about the menstrual cycle,

And he did, and he sent it in, and the editor snapped it up. How many of you can say their first publication was in *Sulfur*?

I had to submit again and again,

It was like stuffing oysters into a parking meter,

again and again, with those 25 cent stamps,

but for Chris, instant fame,

O golden boy of the dark red blood cave.

5.

"I've taken to this far too easily, haven't I," sighs the naked British boy in Travis Mathews's clip

On his stomach in a heap of Laura Ashley, long legs pushing away from the wallpaper. Bedclothes slithering, winking.

I've taken far too easily to the path that has opened before me like a shop with no doors,

He has been in the wind for yonks, the wispy stuttering wind,

His cradle a sheet under his belly, his butt like tongs, my mind a salad.

It has been a wreck for yonks,

I'm like a British milliner,

My hat on purple

I tried to stay true to my mother, my country, my ID but the ball's in your court,

for I've taken to this far too easily, haven't I? I who pretended not to know how to curry favor, to walk a straight line,

I've dropped my aitches like the little girl at your wedding, parading and crumbling petals in 'er clean little 'and.

Balls in your court, balls in your mouth, Steve, I leave it to you,

this palace of fine 'earts,

Your cafeteria,

The Kunsthalle Karl Jaspers. "Alone, I sink into gloomy isolation—only in community with others can I be revealed!—in the act of mutual discovery."

Cyborg Events

Matt Damon flat on his back, a needle in the skin between his thumb
and hand, and when he awakes,

a metal apparatus like a cross has been thrust into and out of his
nervous system, in *Elysium*, the aspirational luxury satellite all plebes
hope to reach one day.

He's Max, speaks Spanish,

with an Italian name, apparently the only

white man in Los Angeles in 2054,

the populace, unruly, is looking to get out.

When I got my arms and legs embedded I could crush walnuts

with my nuts, I was a rampage on legs,

a tripod shoots out of my butt should I choose to sit,

These, the cyborg events of my lifetime, were rubbed into my cortex
like lanolin long ago, in childhood, when I knew one girl, and one
nun, and wrote their names on my skin with my nail.

F + M with a halo over our names,

I guess it's female and male, and the halo I meant as "forever,"

Funny how I died, but the cyborg events came true, Jack,

everyone became a citizen and Obamacare chambers flew down to
earth in the belly of a big white bird.

It was on a treaty we signed,

with the human figments that became Jodie Foster in extremis, sort of
a Jacobean period for the star I once loved the best?

Felt I could do anything—

—yet the power of correction remained with the state.

Skirt

In the future our face falls off like our

Skirt.

Underneath the dermis and the epidermis a wide, flat, interstitial space takes the shape of a mask,

A catcher's mask,

if there was a catcher in Venice, Italy.

In fact if Holden Caulfield had a secret robot type watcher, trailing him, spying on his every move, it would be me behind that hickory tree in Central Park,

that hickory wind that's calling me home.

Where do I go, I can't stalk this boy forever, he'll think I'm a phony.

What do I do, am I even a person? I mimic the humans who walk the streets of New York in their business suits, their khakis, their polo shirts, their human hands clutching bats or briefcases,

my hand is made from cows' teeth, the knuckles of bark,

hickory wind as I pass my palm to my nose,

between my cows' teeth I see Holden pass now, his adorable face smug with disdain,

erasing all the graffiti I put up to enrage him.

I was like, fuck that little sister of his! In the factory we didn't get little usses, nossir *nothing* was

small, there was just a zillion copies of our selves, the teeth and metal ligatures thrown every which way like a potter gone mad.

I'd quit this job but,

he's so expressive,

—Think I'm learning something, watching him shove his fists into the pockets of his jeans,

—strange garment of blue, with funny cuffs and what look like robot studs in the stiff cloth.

Soft Art I-VI

SOFT MACHINE

Soft-serve ice cream dropping, in a twist, soft stalactite, from steel
  mouth overhead

into sugar cone, plop,

and there I was looking up at it, chocolate, vanilla,

William Burroughs's typewriters turning into meat

meat laughing at him, sneering,

should have bought him to Carvel, to Dairy Queen,

The liquid chocolate hardens onto the soft cold peak.

hides not in the minute but rather glories in the hour,

in the space of reformation.

It takes its sweet time in this tumble dry bed, which thou shall work as the water of the spheres.

Wet mattress, wild thyme, coriander, damp, mum.

Shakespeare said there are “sermons in stones, books in

the running brooks,” just get out more, he seemed to be urging us, blow the stink off—

like JFK with his war for fitness, for youth.

A single look at the packed parking lot of the average high school will tell us what has happened

to the traditional hike to school that helped to build young bodies . . .

The Soft American

His own back broken he needed to have sex six times a day to relieve it.

BABY'S BREATH

Soft as a baby's bottom, can you even

say that any more, or is the culture now more rigid, after Michael Jackson and

And flowers tumbling out of a doorway, deep violets whispery with fur,

His face a mask of velvet and vetiver,

    alone in the shadows of what's his name, French anti-hero of Dadaist times,

oh yeah Fantômas.

SOFT ANSWER

soft answer turneth away Ruth.

Asawa.

Interned, Japanese camp, Black Mountain, fabric artist and beloved old lady in San Francisco,

children try to catch her hand as her motorcade sallies down Market

Then when she dies at 87, the Apple store

tries to expand its Union Square acreage by tearing down her ugliest work, the bronze fountains built into its side

I don't know, there's a soft art which inflames the senses,

and then there's you and me lying on our love together.

TAINTED LOVE (SOFT CELL)

You were the cheese cells in the
curd, the whey, the pit in the cherry,

when you went to sleep you
took your dream in a secret
chamber, it was the night sky,
thick as thunder,

It was the place where they invented
aspirin, insulin, formarin—all the drugs
they give you, everything ending with "in,"
in that pink chamber,
bars fitted in the windows,

Big soft factory and
rubber belts on your pretty tan line,
a crimson stain, spreading
hard line of pain on
sit spot of vacancy

I gave you all a boy could give you

THE SOFT TALKERS

But in America they called it *An Air That Kills*,

nothing delicate for the US, just get right down to death,

whereas in England you're led through the mumbles, the lies,
soft talking. Polite table chat like Lady
Mary would have with Papa

servants deferring around them, laying knives and forks, slapping each
other's wrist sub rosa,

In the room downstairs, anguished gay valet plots to destroy them,

all he wanted to do was give that Turk a blowjob, but

Lady Mary killed him with her Mitford thigh ecstasy,

An air that kills across vast old dining room, where once Shirley
MacLaine tried jazzy-cum-tap tap dance number on Ivor
Novello, knees up, Mother Brown . . . he gay too . . .

and Father Brown, so paradoxical, one ear cocked to God.

He the Little Flower of my way.

Yellow Clay

Pasolini

First, after the spots in the Sun
the twenty-seven holes in the coronal
Then, the meeting in the hotel
with a man in a cape only more discreet   Visconti

First, look at the blackened scar
an elbow like a piece of macaroni
Then on the plate
I nearly came while I was looking   "No Hands"

First, both ways, crossing the
street to the traffic island
Then a big van painted multicolor
hippie style, a tiger across it   The 60s

First, why don't you shave
your filthy face is burnt with oil
Then you could maybe eat
a bit of fruit like maybe, my little guava   foreplay

First in the Mezzanine Palace
of the ancestors
Last on my list of like
required reading, get it?   Lovecraft

Mallarmé's "Sea Breeze"

My skin's all peeling, ugh, my tats melt from my forearms,

into the illegible wax sperm flat on shower floor.

Let's you and me follow the gulls drunker than Onan's daughters

deep into the vault of violet sky. Hey, sea breeze.

Nothing, not even the gated community of Sea Ranch

can stop us from jumping off the ruinous cliff

into the dark! Quick, Laure, blow out the candles.

What's that white unicorn-esque maquette in your palm?

You feed it honey from your glass menagerie?

Just quit this life! Little canoe, tied down with twizzle sticks,

swivel your bow towards exotic everywhere:

"Kiss today goodbye, and point me towards tomorrow."

Cover my departing footprints with hankies in the sand.

And maybe the oars of life, dipping into the Liffey,

were only mother's name for life's adversities?

A change is as good as a rest, she used to moan,

but nothing ever changes bar the sailor boy's birthstone.

Get Outta My Way (A Sestina)

As a party game, we used to ask, like Kylie Minogue: "What's the worst thing that could happen to you?"

I don't play that game no mo. I'm lucky I guess, but is there such a thing as occurrence without agency? Inside the belly of the sestina,

I survived just like Elaine Stritch,
The life inside the sestina of Scotch,
Bringing those key words back again and Stritch,
At the close of the sestina, I'll have a Scotch.

She sang about all the things she survived, did Elaine Stritch,
The ladies who lunch, J. Edgar and Herbert Ho-oo-oover, and Scotch,
Plugged in my bowels a silicon of pewter, rub it, it will stritch,
What's the worst thing that could happen to Scotch?
To be trapped inside this sestina with the Memphis blues a Stritch,

If so I could be the poster boy for Scotch

Now I've showed you what I'm made of, Stritch.

Now I've showed you what I'm made of, Scotch, Stritch.

Reading Brian Boyd's *Vladimir Nabokov*

Game to Gunmetal: the volume came unwilling from the stolid row of Brittannicas with a satisfying "blump," and Boyd took a hazy pleasure inserting a clipped finger between two of its faux-gold pages to open the book on his father's pre-Czarist desk. 14th edition, Volume 10.

He turned his eyes towards the negotiating sunset. Tall French windows revealed a row of plane trees cunningly planted to obscure the ash-filled valley. A softening pried his mandible from his maxilla almost to eye-level with the page. "Game," he was disappointed to find, had nothing in any of its columns on *Call of Duty 4: Modern Warfare* (2007), and not even a squib on insouciant *Mario Kart 64* (1996), which had much eased his difficult childhood with its pretty pink leaves, purple bats, green propellers a-twirl to dreamy synthesizer beat. No, "Game" apparently meant the pleasure some men found in trapping rabbits and elks in forests and blowing their brains out, carting them home strapped to boxy range rovers.

It seemed that the book was well titled, for there must be few applications of "Game" to which "Gunmetal" would not come as a spankingly well chosen appositive.

Secret Lives

in a secret project space,

Chicago, tonight, your fate is on the wall.

I flew out of the west to greet you in this limited zone,

I brought cupcakes and pot from the Haight to the Mission.

Secret lives in a post-gay economy,

where I could marry you—or you—tomorrow,

and in the space of an hour could lose my female hormones

to a non-matriculating major of Penn.

Up on the Miracle Mile I gazed at the wall,

where all the great buildings and freaks of the world got kid-

napped to this site, on location, the Taj Mahal, the Eiffel Tower,

the Sphinx, so I thought of you, again grew depressed.

My tears won't stop, you can put all the green ink in that

river thing. In France they call what I've got the

secret de Polichinelle, the thing everyone's got on

Matthew and Olivia, but I can't say their names.

Another life has other lives to live.

"He Was a Writer"

Do you know that song by Cilla Black, "He Was a Writer"? Crazy time

time track, track tells a story in accents loud flashy as Cher's "Gypsies, Tramps, and Thieves,"

Let me take you into Cilla's world, working in a posh bookshop, where all is orderly, quiet; good neat people step in, like Mrs. Dalloway, order books and flowers, depart, leave us humming. All the greater the shock when one night at closing time rain splashes the streets of Sloane Ranger—bells jingle at the bookshop door and Cilla looks up, there he stands—in a tattered jacket—

He was a writer, from Cooper Union, and his first love would always be his pen! Read, "penis,"

Read, "Lord Byron," "limp," "smoulder," "Satan,"—

there was magic in every word he said . . . They tumble into a tumbulultuous clench, but she and books in general are too small for him to stick with long, soon she wakes, he's gone, and she goes back to her tidy life, cardigans, pleated skirts, ivory brooches. Oh Antonio,

you promised when you walked me home,
that one day I would read your book,

Cilla strains her ears, she loved him, at the kitchen table, she blows kisses in his ears. Papers scattered and crumpled, Cilla I'm trying to narrate!

Then one day long after a shipment arrives at Montgomery's Bookstore,

She opens the stack, the dedication is right where she hoped it would be, but on the back cover your picture stares at me, your tattered jacket, your magic, your being gone, as if you never cared for me, though you wanted Shirley Bassey dead but me alive somehow—

Sometimes it takes a quiet woman to make a young man blussssshhhhhhh

You were a writer, and your narration was the sweetest ever told.

Mosquitoes

Mosquitoes in flight

Tiny wings batting the air

Eggs into egg cream

Fennel

Fennel in meadow

Scent pongs across land and sea

to San Francisco

Fuzz

Dandelion fuzz

clouds face of pretty baby

Sleep crowds the eyelids

Tablet

So there I was with this tablet, see,

White and hard like a pool ball, shiny,

But small, I could swallow it, it cured my headache,

And there was a yellow tablet, they gave me to write on.

Write down your impressions of Rome, of lunch, or poverty,

All these different things I had thoughts on,

When all I wanted to do was see *My Fair Lady*.

Why these two different tablets, have they a root in common, Professor Higgins, or what's your name, Colonel Pickering was it?

I'll ask someone who knows something,

And in the meantime I'm seeing lines,

Lots and lots of lines on this tablet,

I'm following the trail to my tongue,

It is making me rue the day I brought my lot to Fresno Street . . .

The Gifts of San Francisco

These

were the gifts of San Francisco, the popsicle

invented by a boy not even 12 years old, in a heat wave;

the Mai Tai, like a chapter from Drew Cushing's novel

of boy brothels in the days of the Barbary Coast;

cioppino, crab soup of the Genovese fishermen who

swam, like Mark di Suvero, through the towers of the Golden Gate Bridge—white thick hot mass of potash in bowl;

Irish coffee, a splash of brandy in java, perks you up as it knocks you down;

thc fortunc cookie, poem, warning, ransom

wrapped into thin dough, you will meet a dark stranger;

Crab Louis, named after Louis Quatorze? Louis CK? Louis Armstrong? Louis Nye, crabfaced specter of my childhood,

crazy Frank Gorshin-like villain of afternoon TV;

Pisco Punch with that little hint of piss in its very

name, oh sure, yes, shake me up a dozen, bartender;

chicken Tetrazzini, they hailed her at the opera,

held her aloft by her legs and arms in a torchlight procession of chicken, of angels;

green goddess dressing, not the protoplasmic creature of Robert Graves's desiring, but

a woman like Alice Waters in the slow food living foods movement,

her arms stained with light and chlorophyll;

the Martini, they served them at our poets theater intensive performance in Vancouver,

but instead of vermouth, Lee offered lemon-lime soda, delicious and wry,

like the late Elaine Stritch, next day it's pretzels and beer;

that seems clear

Rice-a-Roni, bell clang on hill top, swoops of brakes unfurling down Nob Hill, I longed

to be in the TV commercial like a boy in a brothel, red, gold;

Hang Town Fry, before the end of the poem I will know what it is, the image shall descend on me like a halo,

like a hey-hey-low, and

It's-it, graham crackers and chocolate, dipped over ice cream, part time paradise, like its id, and these,

the gifts of San Francisco, I extend to the ego, the superego, the colors and germs of your generosity. Come Freudian constructs,

I am tired of my self and of hobbling these lists,

in infinite reconstruction throw ashore your appetites,

want all of them to unravel under my skin, like that Korean movie we saw,

The Host, a little drop of poison and an alien sea lion erupts from river downtown

in Seoul, chaos ensues, family implodes, a hundred things dissolve their hope in acid;

my gifts come softer than those.

Ruined city under the apoplectic heel of the eel . . . in the blink of time in which the match head catches, can you see its

halo

Pink Narcissus

Pink Illusions

I've got these freaky angels
With white wings in my
Pink illusion house

They feather my walls with "rache,"
"revenge" in German

And I was so close!
That's what kills me,

to a heaven mad with flower petals and zigzag
papers, bangles and beads, the dream
of the warrior, and then to find out

like a snap of salts

it was only a ruse, of pink illusions
I was never going to be a player

Along the river the fountain plays,
And Sapphic songs are sung,
But not for me

Water Colors

In Brooklyn we flipped Necco Wafers with our thumbnails from the table's edge to a glass of water standing between us in the diner booth

> Watch closely as wafer after wafer gives up its bruised secret of water colors, pale pink, dusty orange, cocoa brown, and that green, the green of pistachio ice cream. . . We have come so far that

In order to get to you, Jeanne, what a strange path I had to take!

> —so long to come to you

> In the passageway I squeezed past his enormous brim and into the porthole where, lay waiting, like a snake crawling from the left edge of the page to the right, then bounding back

"Pour aller jusqu'à toi, quel drôle de chemin il m'a fallu prendre."

That was where I was going when the call came

to shut down the shop

> In Flatbush my grandfather ruled the halls of Bushwick High, a ruler in his hand, not your regular 12 inch ruler but an 18 incher, students quaked when they saw him come your way, the fear whitening their eyebrows and sideburns like Macaulay Culkin

This was the principal's grandson of the royal house of Killian

when taken, the medicine goes up the down staircase,

> The side effects closed on my nose

Clock ticks on

It took me such a long time to catch this busy coach to Yuma

where, we were on a Greyhound bus and Robin Thomas, the perfect name for him, slept on my lap all night long his head piled high with dreams and water colors

Test Shots

Ed sent me a picture of my dumb, insensate face, eyes glazed and dull, as though life were a TV and I was thinking about watching it. I could have recognized myself instantly, since that image is what I look like to myself—I don't know about the rest of you, but when I think about what I look like that's what I see, that's what I would draw. I thanked him for the photo and then he said he had more, some were not just of my face—they formed a whole range of, well, there I was, nude, in his living room, drunk, nervous, trying to act nonchalant but flunking. I could remember doing this shoot and Ed trying to talk me down, trying to relax me. And me afraid, thinking I was overweight, thinking first that I was too small, then that I'd get hard, it was a headache-making dilemma, but in general I was trying to back into the wallpaper hoping it would eat me, cover me, and praying I wouldn't have to uncross my legs.

Sandcastle

Wet sand at the beach, Sandcastle,
And on the rocky beaches of San Francisco,
you can only make a condo out of the sand here,

in *Ulysses*,
Why should no man starve in the deserts of Arabia?
Because of the sand which is there.

The milk rolls in, great curves of milk,
authentic Pacific ocean blue,
built on sand like my apartment on Minna Street

During the earthquake we shook and rolled
building castles in the air,
an authentic Joni Mitchell moment I couldn't stomach,
I felt sick and puked my lunch on the steps, sitting down fast

feeling the earth roll under my legs,

"How came the sandwiches there?
The tribe of Ham was bred there and mustered."

as years ago I dared my new friend, Buzzy's straight friend,
into Long Island Sound with me, way after midnight,
nearly moonless night, warm, with a buzz on,

I'll leave my underwear on, he said,
yes do, I said, I don't want you uncomfortable,

Then dashed, like the witch of the low tide, into the surf,
leaving him to follow my bare forked body,
if he would, fine, if he wouldn't, that's okay,

He was from Moscow, Idaho, and had never
seen the ocean before,
and this was not the ocean.

First Cover

First cover your arms with suntan lotion then exacerbate the way you feel by dipping your torso into the tight red and black matador outfit James Bidgood has stayed up all night in his tiny room sewing for you—a trick jacket, shirt and bolero tie combination that's really all one garment and fits like kid glove. This is the sequence in which you, the matador who kills the bulls, enters the arena without pants but splendid from the waist up and, if the truth be told, splendid from the waist down. Noël Coward wrote his song "Matelot" for his lover Graham Payn when their love was still new and Payn still straight; that song, somehow mournful and glum, has stayed playing in James Bidgood's head all night as he sews spangle after spangle across the broad shoulders of your matador top.

A little bird fluttered outside the tenement window, came to rest on the soot-covered sill. The bird that whispered to Bidgood all night long, "A matelot is different than a matador." Those voices that plagued him, that infused him with doubt. "A matelot is some kind of sailor." "No, no, that can't be true, I'm halfway done with the costume—and you will be here in the morning if the heroin will let you." "Then why do you think the song says, 'Here within my arms you'll sleep, Sailor from the deep.'" "No, no, I won't listen." Over his ears she jammed two hands, hands stinging with needles and thread and sequins. "Don't torture me with doubt." "Why do you think the song says, 'Matelot, matelot, where you go my heart will follow, when you go down to the sea.' He doesn't say, when you go down to the bullring." When that bird had done moving its beak Bidgood was in tears, and your skintight matador top sparkled with tears like the water of some distant Catalan spring.

Apache

His cap looked like a bicycle seat, Apache
said to be a dangerous dance for tough louts in Marseilles
dragging their dames behind them like cavemen in some
Nicole Eisenman allegory of modern urban social pressure and the transparency of nostalgia—
Think of how many swear by Nabokov, still, the absolute perfection of the word crossed by the smack of translation, one is always moved by how Russians suffer here, where the language is too small for their rivenings.
Were you ever in love with red stripes on your pants,
or were you teary-eyed then, your scalp ablaze,
dragged along sawdust-slick barroom floor in the provinces, where he was an Apache and you a kind of brass spittoon with attitude.
"Splat!" It is the sound of the sixties,
Diane Linkletter from a great height,
Ana Mendieta from a great height,
Sherlock Holmes fell from the Reichenbach Falls, that great soul stilled forever or at least until the adventure of the empty house.
"Splat!" Apache hatchet flat against the fat cat's mat hat. Donny Hathaway, 15th floor of the Essex House in New York, the windows rattling with soul, his beautiful body wrecked on the courtyard.
Hart Crane, Weldon Kees, look up at me and take pity on a man so patchy.
Crane, Kees, from the sea's dark bottom your mocking glances comfort me, you have gone to the place of apache.

Huck Finn

Alone on a raft, disguised as a baron and a count—
Accounts of their subsequent travels vary.
Very inconspicuous were the American flags of the men,
Many more patriots lived at that time than today.
Day by day, the pastures sauntered, lucid greenery, river banks ignited in daffodil yellow
Yellow sheen on the silver spoon he bit down on, a coating of saffron bitter on his tongue.
Tonga idol on the wild boys' raft, almost as if floating away, the stone sat alone.
All one ever needs in life is a ten-cent cigarette.
Rhett Butler stood there, jet black from the boots up.
Up which drainpipe are you planning your getaway?

Get away from my innocence, it is not to be trifled with.
With rainbows on the rolling yellow river now only mist, a
    pixelated, humid frost I could write my initials in
In the Civil War time we had not a chunk of bread in the house
How's that going for you, racing your destiny, being alone?

Evil

He is nowhere near the knife.
He couldn't be much further away.
He took seven pill handfuls—
Seven steps to suicide.

Se7en with Brad Pitt, evil!
Gwyneth Paltrow's head in a hatbox,
What's his name, Morgan Freeman,
yes, totally rigorous and tart.

I want a pink ice cream cone,
Something to take my mind off evil,
to pay our rebuffs to Satan.
Maybe a feathery, green-eyed bird.

Willow Tree

Flames shadow your face, your cousinry.
Smell that burning engine? Above us tied garlands of ribbon imitate the kind of green love I felt for you,
jealous of the food and drink your mouth let in,
of the shit your asshole squeezes out,
for I could not be close to you as they.
Strips of green ribbon tied any which way dangle from the sky, or from the top of a willow tree,
They suggest branches as I whisper in your ear, you are drunk Richard Loeb and can't resist me when I touch you
The hidden grove is a patchwork of pink hearts sewn together, pink hearts puffy with potpourri and smelling sort of feral
I will commit a crime with you, willow tree, if for every crime I commit you grant me two or three sexual acts. I've got my penis between your legs, practicing some mouth perversions
Grow dizzy when you nod your head, and we will burn a car together,
I will cover your breast with moss,
You will be my second cousin.
Now I've showed you what I'm made of

Now I've showed you what I'm made of

Pink Narcissus

The wallpaper that bumped your ass as you leaned into the wall I later cut from its gluespecie and kept as a drain, my tongue inserted into each of its numerous creases

Gay wallpaper, daffodils bright as the sun over Ljubljana in springtime, a pattern of crocuses 102 centimeters from the polished floor,

That is the space your ass kissed

Those plaid inches of compression

Solemn Slovenian boy, with your cock out, turn away from flowered wall,

come to me butt first, let me pull cheap Soviet made jeans down from over your swelling architubure,

Introduce your ass to my lap, show Mr. Cock the door, he's not wanted any more.

Wallflower of mixed register, grind like the boy who sits on coal fire, trying to put out the fire with the anal mucus you proheave in times of plenty,

In state school

In the prison of your Levis,

hidden from authority of the gaze, evading panopticon,

Why? Because I like to eat you out,

tart candy in ornate dish,

let your asshole speak to my tongue's tip, my dithyrambic inprinciplements.

Scrabble tile with the score of ten on opposite corners,

I will move you up and down till I find a sentence where that hole attains meaning,

In the meantime your cock must be cold,

Put a sock on it sky boy, tell it a ghost story, soothe it to sleep, let it lie, like the strips of red and black licorice displayed in Caspian Sea port windows when the sailors come to town on passes of so-called liberty. And the girls call out, "Licorice! Get yer limp, thin, red, black twisty braids of licorice here!"

Gilded Cage

Let a restaurant into your comb,
and be the woman of your dreams.
Drama walks warily towards bad access,
seceding Dab-Dab, the duck from the Doctor Dolittle books,
and other ducks succeeding.

The success that curled the heart of our duck.

Made him half blind with jealousy.

There was a retro tip to Ken
as he climbed the sexual pyramid to my crib.
Birch-built sauna in Scandinavian poet land,

Scandinavian, wasn't he, Sophie?

Wonton soup rising like steam, boys,

He was the last fuse of the Amoko,
Karma chameleon, you stood there still,
when all the wardens caved to Third Nations,
and you watched the men's mogul heat in round two.

Brown-eyed boy with yobbo cut,
Tuck your chair deeper into your gratin.
The ratings have fallen, like steam in reverse, mates.

And Dab-Dab runs amok, smoked crockery frock hoisted low.

Bidgood Bidgood Bidgood

on wall blood spatters as it spatters on farmhouse door ; boy's teeth whiter than milk ; teeth speckled with spinach ; green spinach on the movie set of the day he was eviscerated ; cut hollers director Wassaghi ; spinach on teeth ; thugs move quickly towards boy on bed ; above bed white and pink panels of wallpaper ; poodles bark ; grey, black and white poodles on wallpaper an evil pink ; below frilly bed of ingenue girl's thighs white and concupiscent ; frilly nightgown in Jane Russell pink ; boy sits up abruptly as if woken from sleep ; woken from dream of camera ; red eye of camera blinks once then twice then after long pause one more time as if dying ; red eye fades into pink eye of dying light circle ; blood spatters on bedroom wall as it has spattered on every movie set since days of Méliès brothers in France ; epic France of the impressionists ; no what were those brothers called ; abruptly thugs grab boy by shoulders ; fingers slide up into armpits ; armpit hair of boy a silken factory of worms ; rough fingers of young thugs run through each armpit of boy gripping muscle ; yank young lad to feet ; assistant director points gun at feet of boy ; thugs stand clear ; boy drops to bed ; dances ; shots ring out ; air filled with stink of cordite ; boy rubs ass on tamarind tree ; bedroom filled with tamarind trees each marked by fear scent of boy ; cut repeats director Wassaghi ; blood flies up like language patterns ; marks pink walls of poodle as girl's screams vibrate and pierce still movie set ; day for night ; lighting dim on pillow though harsh on boy's feet now bare since thugs have taken his bedroom slippers from him ; each slides a bedroom slipper up and down his own belly ; each yanks open waistband on thug trousers far enough away from tummy to insert stolen slipper in the direction of cock ; pubic area received slipper toe ; stolen slipper toes erect the cocks of standing thugs tugging footwear inside flies of pants ; up and down motion betrays nationalism of actors versus directors ; boy's face panicked white ; freckles large and looming ; director announces traditional last meal prepared for boy about to die in service of making movie ; waiter appears to take order ; pad in hand, pencil in hand ; boy tears ; no no no not last meal ; I'm only 21 for the Lord's sake ; would you like cake or steak ; bourbon based bouillabaise or Kentucky fried chicken ; we get all kinds ; nothing's too outré or banal for last meal of man about to die ; boy temporizes ; what was Kenneth Anger's last meal begs boy ; he hasn't been killed yet replies director ; impatient thugs lift boy from edge of mattress and shuck off pajama pants like banana skin peeling down pale legs ; one hand hides privates as he tries to think ; what should be his last meal ; perhaps a dish so complicated to make it would give him extra hours of life ; life in Hollywood ; may I call my agent he murmurs ; hands filling up with privates ; through chinks in fingers his erection swells ; shaved cock glistening with suntan lotion and precum ; its head too big for palm ; scrotum in mouth of thug ; buttocks parted by thug two with rough hands on which the skin is thicker than stained canvas of gloves ; thug bites exposed asshole of trapped condemned boy ; grease on teeth from hidden grease of condemned boy star of James Bidgood feature ; boy thinking about last meal and which meal less humiliating to request ; junior high school lessons still paramount in consciousness of distressed boy ; director Wassaghi claps hands twice ; thug one freezes jaw full of balls ; thug two continues nibbling licking and biting greased up anus ; girl dresses in wardrobe ; makeup artists approach bed with small white towels ; pat away sweat from boy armpits ; smear cold seminal fluid from five previously dispatched boys on freckled forehead and snub nose of new condemned boy ; he smells the jissom ; jissom of a handful of dead boys ; makeup artists apply chapstick to erection in covering fingers of boy ; chapsticked cockhead gleams in camera's white eye ; profile of master James Bidgood manifests itself à la spiritualist phenomenon in mirror fitted on the side of the gun in the gunbelt of thug one ; reflection of master costumier, photographer, scenarist ; boy Huck Finn introduced to thug dildo on the count of ten ; ten ; nine ; eight ; seven ; six ; five ; and what is to be your last meal boy ; four ; three ; Quarter Pounder I guess whatever is simpler ; two ; one ; zero ; push cries director ; push push push ; spray of blood jumps from ruined asshole onto pink wall of poodles who seem to relish new coating of iodized blood of red boy next door ; now lying in sodden pink sheets on huge Hollywood bed hardly breathing ; Quarter Pounder applied to his lips by union makeup artists ; he takes a nibble

Valentine

Valentine

It says here that suspended
animation's come a long
way since bygone Lazarus/
Passover Plot times

It says Walt Disney never
really died he's lying
on a bed of chilled cubes
somewhere in Anaheim

taking what his associates
laughingly call a
holiday on ice.

If I only had life to live
I would live it with a blond like you.
Frozen roses are frozen red,
frozen violets are frozen blue.

Marnie and Monotheism

for Robert Glück

Colored pictures of baby Jesus pointing at his genitals
which I think are pretty spooky anyhow
no matter who it is who is the painter;

but first the problem is that nobody sees them
it is a quandary in that you cannot explain them to
those who say OH EVERY BABY DOES THAT, and these exist.

Who are these people who are so blind, Bob?
why do they think that about babies—
I have begun the crusade against their ways.

Still when baby Jesus has his one red spot
glowing and blinding, a spiral of cream silk and fire
affects the eye like Matisse leaning into the doorway

of this taverna I picture, then there shall be this stigma
attached to really seeing what's in front of one's nose,
it's like the curse of having children—having,

that's to say, to see them do little but radiate
spiritual pride for a pointless and ugly scratch
with a Latin name, so safes get broken into

The mother of Marnie, a London whore in the blitz
stringing a child inside a sofa and fucking a white man
and killing him for GI V-medal. I believe in Freud,

who else would imagine that this could deliver
like a suppurating tick that kind of delay
that could make one, God, Sean Connery, love you forever?

The banker who takes you out to his yacht and xxxxx
xxxx, the weather that, aloof from the sun, exists to break
rain and the stars into XY number of wet glass shards;

were it due to only *one strand* of painting myth or
tradition they might then comprehend. But two! People feel
their eyes crossing when they look both ways so no pain . . .

I don't mean "xxxxx xxx," my dear, that's a gesture
of rhetoric, only a code that broken down like Bob Kaufman
means this: that there's a person out there to address

with a mind to be changed—maybe in the hinterlands—;
he or she reading this poem, we determine, can slowly be made
flawless like Pasolini or, like Tippi Hedren, human.

Magi staring like the dickens at the genitals, and
even Mary like, touching, like she's a nitwit, like but this is
all in *October*: 25 and written up by Leo Steinberg

and the other attribution is to *mise-en-scène*,
a flat cardboard reel of Hitchcock rotogravure, written by
someone so hot that no one today recalls his or her name.

Tottering Bridge, Exploding Bomb

Tottering bridge, a bomb burst
under you and seized your supports,
reducing you to splinters. Once
you'd carried kings to queens,
costers to market—now you're a
heap of toothpicks. Still your
presence is felt: every time we
call each other up & make dates
to meet, we're replicating the
functions you used to perform.

Exploding bomb, once you'd gone off
& destroyed tottering bridge I
began to feel pity for you. Who
can imagine your bland beginnings
in an alley workshop, three parts
metal, one part fizz, without
regretting you're now all ash?
I never did like that old wood bridge—
he was so phallic, so imperious.
You and he now share a common state
of fulsome, bygone pastness. In a
few years I'll join you both.

Pickpocket

Last night whistling I passed
by their alley, saw them in a
sidelong blink of light from
traffic, a speeding car, then
I went home. Dreamed of
gold skies, black money. I
felt so stupid, to talk
about them feels stupid. I'm
the sullen red Sun.

Bernadette leans from tenement
windows, sailors keep searching
world after world for
Bernadette, and her arms
are black, her outstretched
proffered palms all milky.
From them coins drop into
Pickpocket's pockets freely.

Pickpocket's face is pocked, his
arms are pocked. I threw
his face in a lake to make it
ripple, he smokes a
cigar to an orange hot hole in
his face, a glow, at night
the Sun's a kid brought behind
the woodshed and abased.

Jealous Roommate

"And why do you write?" she said to me.
She's everyone from A to Z.
"I write," I said, "because it's fun,
Because, like Jell-O,
I have been invented."

Leave It Alone, It's All Gone

Let's have a drink, Barrett
Barrett, you're too skinny to be a nanny.
I do wish you'd stop yapping at Barrett all the time—you try to find another like him.
They used to call me Basher Barrett, I was quite a driller.
Oh hello Barrett—just getting a bit of air in the garden.
I thought you'd be uncertain, Barrett.
Barrett, Barrett, come down here! My dear Barrett, you're just a little upset because you're losing the game.
I'm not staying here in a place where they just chuck balls in your face.

Don't Look Inside

When I'd lived with you for a week
I felt the backbone in my back start to freak.
O lover with your turquoise hair,
Your funny British accent, and the dresses you wear

I went to the store and bought some food
You went to Nassau where the waiters were rude
Honey, you're a person who hates to not come
I bought some food and you wanted some.

Looks good—doesn't look bad—
Looks small—don't look inside.

I met a lady with a little white dog
She told me I could help her give it a walk in the park.
I got took, she got shook;
We were accosted by a man with a hook.

Oh lover don't you misunderstand me now,
I'm not talking about what you use for an alibi
Don't put me down for being hard to play with.
I used to look at your face in the mirror and say,
"Don't look inside."

I saw a hurdy-gurdy man with a monkey,
He said, "Why don't you grow up and be a man?"
I said, "It's a wonder I'm not like you, with a monkey on my back."
I wonder if he knew what I meant . . .
I wonder sometimes if you're a hitter,
A set of nerves with a built-in stricture
A stab—a winding stair—an organ grinder
Or are you a person with a heart on a stretcher?

And oh lover when you take me in your arms and tell me
Your little daughter will be four next Tuesday
I want you to take my hands to scratch me

Anything you please that you figure won't be too bourgeois,
That will wake me up.

When I was little, Daddy took me to the farm.
He wanted to show me the cornstalks, and the cornsilk and the
 livestock and the mower
He was talking about the way people mate.
He said it's like when you ice skate.
If so it's over thin ice I'm skating
You let me touch you when you're masturbating
Oh Daddy you remind me of a terrible thing,
Oh lover, you became when you tried to sing.
You lay in bed with your breath, a form of paradisal fecklessness,
Then you cried out and opened wide,
And told me not to look inside

Think of me, you said, as a Pandora's box,

Saturday
Saturday
Saturday

You were mean to me,

And Sunday, I stood on a line,
To ask you to be mean to me.

Monday
Monday
Monday
Was just like any other day

But someday, we said,
We'll lie in green pastures someday . . .

endlessnature

Coloring Book

I was coloring in the picture, thinking of how I always liked to stay between the lines

Or did I like that especially, or was it always that I wanted the gold star certain teachers would award me?

Pictures of geese, easy to color; pictures of rabbits in complicated house-dresses? No thanks

Early on Boy learns the easy way out

I was coloring in the picture, and the crayons seemed unresponsive to the facts of a goose, the facts of the Boy

There's Santa. What color is Santa? Kind of red, but not the red in the box. And his face was red, I sat on his lap. Saw the sheer Irish weight of Scotch in his cheeks

In despair, I stood and tried picking on the other children's crayons,

swiping them into my pockets, turning to crime I guess.

There, on the teacher's desk, a packet of stars

gleaming gold, like the mirrors of Shanghai,

And a little voice screamed within my brain. "Take them, take the stars, take back the materials of specialized labor, take the applause. Why make the thing when you can take the reward?" It was done in a minute, embarked on a colorful career.

"A/ butterfly"

A
butterfly was passing by,
could you see its wings, orange with dust?
Do you need help adjusting your vision?
Eventually we all find our butter-
Fly

Exhausted Autumn

Eyes on the Prize

Yet I'm calling you,
My gaze bangs bullets through the vernal air,
but pay no attention,
I'm a slumpateur, hitless, no chance of building.

Eyes on the prize, yet everywhere
I'm drowning with my eyes above me.
The three ring shit list of my master's heart
doth fire away, anent the furore of "Big Top,"

Of the man they call "Big Top."
Look! Black dogs and monkeys circle the tent,
one is holding a scroll in her teeth,
she is the poem Lab.

Eyes on the Prize

The red room of pain and
—now what were you saying?
It was all about the heavy headdress Nature made you wear, through the
        sunlit streets of Stockton.
Eric, tucked into the flower shop, a boy, taking orders on the phone,
        tonight you sit on my armoire, grinning, a gargoyle,
        scars criss crossing your back.

Eyes on the Prize

Been a roller coaster rush, this dying phase,
The year goes by like the brass ring that once I grabbed for,
        Sullen, naked, my genitals bouncing as up I tossed my hair,
            down on the balls of my feet, I was lucky I guess,
  Everything I wanted came to me and I lived till I met you, Arpad,

I was a little depressed, but you caught it worse,
you the chemist who turned to porn, to get out, to get off,
    You brushed the hair of the perfume genius so womanly,
the penny drops, I click on it, I understand,
    love makes servants out of each other. If I could
        I'd mend that chemistry that caught your dick in my hole,
but somehow let you down at the very NY second—
    February sheaf, for Arpad Miklos, in the garden of Chaldea.

Eyes on the Prize

If I were a horse I'd never run out of this track,
I'd keep coming for more of that finish line bullshit.
I'd raise my one hoof and then stumble, a dainty doe, a cod like old baby,
And the jock above me would slide off my back, really polish my fur with his butt, and he'd cry, lady . . .
he—would—cry. Our age, bereft of nobility. How do we get shod here?
Take me to that hot place and turn the anvil over your knee,
    bend with your mind that risky rod till it U's you, in its
        vocal way, sizzling sparks, white blisters on your Rosa parks.

Eyes on the Prize

Christopher,
what was hard was soft,
You ford the fjord at its turbulent fork, moving slowly, pants wet and
        heavy, lunging off your hips, fourth century precursor of
        today's urban youth.
Civic rulers pay you to guide the travelers,
one of whom was the infant Christ.
You did a double take and this ordinary baby *became the infant Christ*
whom *you* bore on orange vinyl, tubular pinks, black stove stacks—
        tucked in your arms, bone dry.

What up Chris? And then
                when I got to you,
You're so—can I even call it "foreign"?—
you failed to understand the sayings, "good sport" and "breaking the ice."
        Was Christ this cold? I'll bet he was, huh? It's not like
you're not a bright lad, but you're from Switzerland.
Brave boy, the future's yours,
        make me something else, and mis-
understand another common US expression,
and carry another big baby across a raging stream, let him change in
                        your colors, let him change in your embrace.

Tony Greene Era

The work of the late, Los Angeles-based artist Tony Greene borrows, often as not, from preceding paint strategies, with a premium on the glowing, the luminous, the grand. Many times we recognize the face or visage of some dreamy man with the Mel Odom looks popular in the Stonewall era of the 1970s. But a glaze lies between us and the man of desire: a glaze profound and dark, which simultaneously lays waste to his beauty, occludes his image. Meanwhile a decorator's hand sprinkles close-ups of unlikely, even surrealistic, emblems, and badges. Pay attention to the frame, too! The artist foregrounds his frames like a Daniel Buren: within them some kind of nightmarish depletion is occurring, rather like the pre-Raphaelites with their portrayals of pale thin women too weak, too lovely, too deluded for this world of pounds and shillings. In his panoply of beauty under siege, Greene skillfully harkens back to earlier models, to Velázquez's lusty and cerebral pictures of Spanish saints, to the lordly Irish criminals of Bacon, the pastel socialites of the Stettheimer sisters—pictures that looked already destroyed, almost gone when you saw them the first time. And then he thought of further ways to problematize the experience of looking at these paintings.

AIDS hard on his heels, Greene completed a prodigious amount of work before his death at age thirty-five in 1990. In the confusing decades that ensued, his art, cherished as it was by his cohort and, later, the subject of a posthumous cult of young artists transfixed by his legend, fell into critical limbo. A handsome catalogue accompanied a traveling retrospective of the work in the months following his death—a show called *Exhausted Autumn*—but after that, one heard very little, then nothing. Was the work too much of its time? At present, the tide seems to be turning. Former Cal Arts students Catherine Opie and Richard Hawkins shepherded their friend's work into the 2014 Whitney Biennial, where Greene was a well-received "discovery;" while in Chicago, independent Iceberg Projects paired Greene's finely worked, mixed media objects alongside pieces by contemporary artists attuned to his influence. Closer to home, at the Mak Center at the ultra-modernist Schindler House in Los Angeles, two other friends of Greene, painters Judie Bamber and Monica Majoli, curated the largest and most interesting Tony Greene exhibition to date. All artists should be so well served by their survivors.

How had he disappeared so completely? As a painter Greene was already fighting what must have been perceived at Cal Arts as a losing battle, one that later became consonant with his personal struggle with AIDS. Cal Arts had many great painters enrolled and on the faculty, and yet it performed as if there was a continual war against painting in favor of other, less time-bound practices. At Valencia everyone knew which way the wind was blowing. If Tony Greene ignored this call, perhaps it was because he already knew what he wanted to do and where he wanted to go. I pulled out the catalogue to *Exhausted Autumn* from my bookcase and leafed through its implacability for awhile.

Its cover is a distinctive green, a deep melancholy forest green—a ripe color, but with a sour tinge, the color you'd feel in your gut after having gobbled down one persimmon too many. I asked the artist Wayne Smith, who designed the Greene catalogue, what color is that, is it forest green? Until that moment, I hadn't even thought of the pun on Tony Greene's name—the "green" catalogue. A "green thought in a green shade," as Andrew Marvell wrote in his poem "The Garden." "I think forest green is the perfect word for that color on the cover," Wayne responded, "though design professionals would call it Pantone 343."

Of the *Exhausted Autumn* catalogue, Smith recalled "liking the gold of the letters and end pages because that color seemed both vital and in a state of decomposition, sort of like Tony's work." For a particular set of artists at the time, gold, like green, represented something liturgical, too, an almost devotional accessorizer. Art was taking a "high" turn, and had seemingly converted to Episcopal or even Roman Catholic in a big way. These were the artists Dennis Cooper and Richard Hawkins had bundled into their heretical *Against Nature* show at LACE in Los Angeles, their "show by homosexual men," which proposed that decadence could be as powerful a structure of resistance as the organized direct political action that critics like Simon Watney and Douglas Crimp had recommended. Crimp pointed out that the *New York Times* still used the word "homosexual," refused, indeed, to print the word "gay,"—so "what happens, then, when Dennis Cooper and Richard

Hawkins also choose to use the term ["homosexual"]? Are they resisting authority or are they acceding to authority?" (I quote from "Good Ole Bad Boys," a lecture at a conference on "AIDS, Art, and Activism" at Ohio State University in March 1989, and later collected in Crimp's *Melancholia and Moralism: Essays on AIDS and Queer Politics*).

Wayne Smith's own project in the 1990 period was his series of realistic prints or paintings, mostly found in thrift stores like St. Vincent de Paul or Goodwill, which he would frame and encase in glass, etching upon each patterns only an alert viewer might notice in the dance of shadows on the picture's surface that revealed, for example, a gloomy, Böcklinesque seascape like the *Isle of the Dead*—with stylized rows of crosses, like those in a veterans' cemetery, etched into its receding horizon. Again, fragments of a romantic, heraldic past, but interrogated into uncomfortable conclusions, a challenge to history's prettier side. A questioning of memory itself—and how it had brought us to this pass.

Smith and Greene share a similarly awkward relationship to the past, with details of an ornamental, pictured memory—sexualized, idealized—floating up into their artworks like Freudian slips—the repressed returning in vengeance. The splendor of something like the image of a torso inlaid by sharply detailed interstices of resin, makes it seem guarded and closed off, like the black cat sealed into the wall in the Poe story. Or, in Greene's case, is the point not the crying, vengeful cat itself, but perhaps the very intricacy of the wall's construction?

On Smith and Greene I detect the influence of their contemporary, the young multimedia artist Nayland Blake (born 1960) whose art displayed an easy familiarity with theory. In his twenties, he was able to demonstrate in his art these lofty suppositions on the meaning of our past. From his work, many of us learned to question the sites, and even more so the substance, of treatment for AIDS. His dazzling hospital installations presented steel and rubber constructions which looked both medical and barbaric at the same time—torture chambers as much as platforms for cure—much like David Cronenberg gave moviegoers all those deadly-looking gynecological instruments in the contemporaneous *Dead Ringers* (1988).

Tony Greene was young when he died, younger than I, so young that I barely remember his face. I was living far from LA, though because we had so many mutual friends he seemed part of my San Francisco world as well. In the 40s, Cold War proponents blamed world tension on the "Comintern," the secret Communist International, the bruited web of red agents / Fifth Columnists that held the fate of the free world in its grasp. In the 60s, the twist became that no, it wasn't Communists, it was the gays—the Homintern, the imaginary conspiracy of gay men and lesbians in the arts and elsewhere who were plotting to destroy Western civilization through the invention of the miniskirt and movies like *Boom!* Queer liberals denied the existence of any such plot, claiming that we were as American and patriotic as the Fourth of July. But by the mid-1980s, the gloves were off, and we mindfully created and enrolled in a Homintern, for we were all sentenced to perish and no one cared. AIDS was then so much a part of life that sometimes days would pass in which one literally thought of nothing else but the disease. Thus Tony Greene's inscribing of AIDS into the materials of his work was something that was happening to me as well, or so I believed.

Two years back, when *Artforum* asked me to write up the Tony Greene recovery project, my editor there said they had invited me because research indicated that Greene and I had published in the same papers and journals. It was the age of zines, the moment when relatively cheap photoduplication seemed to usher in an age when writers and artists might be able to control the means of production—long the dream of the Marxist and anarchist—and not the glossy, expensive productions of today, but a personalized, individual response to the terror around us. The things we published were not meant to last. They were flowers of the pavement, drops of data. Like mercury some of those tiny drops clung together, and that was another working of the Homintern.

Many my age kept address books and crossed off the names of our friends as, one by one, they died in hospice or took their lives or simply disappeared, like elephants crawling away to lose themselves in the jungle. So many names that you couldn't remember all of them. Some were artists, some activists, some both or neither, it was a pool of death deeper than the imagination itself, one that swallowed everything, a kraken.

In 1992, I wrote the catalogue essay for *Without*, an exhibition curated by two local gay artists, Peter Edlund and the late David Cannon Dashiell at San Francisco's nonprofit, artist-run space the Lab, which reflected on many of the absences we felt then. It was a moment in which an unusually large number of partial or vacated pieces were created. While David Wojnarowicz recreated a diorama of the buffalo falling off the cliff in 1994 as a statement about collective free-fall into absence, Félix González-Torres had already become the Pope of Without. On his 1991 MoMA billboards, rumpled sheets and head-dented pillows presented drivers and pedestrians with a silent sob. For the San Francisco *Without* show, Nayland Blake installed a table on which apples were placed one a day until there was no more room on the surface. Blake tweaked the old saying that "an apple a day keeps the doctor away" when, one by one, oxygen worked on these apples till they dissolved into their own rot and juices in nature's ghostliest, richest miasma.

It was a time of fragments as well as absence. I began dreaming of amputation, of waking up to find that a part of my body had been cut away. Later I realized it was me trying to put myself into the mindset of those who were fighting AIDS—deprived, as we saw it, of a future—while vast parts of their "long bodies" (as in Hinduism) are sawn off, disposed of in vats. Loss inside of loss. In this time, when both form and content seemed to have broken down, we placed faith in color. The black and pink and white of the "Silence = Death" logo.

At the 2014 Chicago show at Iceberg Projects, curator John Neff hung a Greene picture, one of his male torsos spectacularly decorated-slash-cloistered by the bright gold and copper signs of a thriving and unstoppable sign-making impulse. In this work—borrowed from Nayland Blake's personal collection—Greene challenges the core conceptions of anger and romantic "feeling." Over and under them twin discourses hover, like swarms of bees at a company picnic. First, the discourse of comedy: the pleasure of having shored so many fragments against this ruin—in Greene's decorative impulse to ornamentation that spreads across the picture's frame. Second, the discourse of discontinuity, the prelinguistic horror that exists within and without representation. Painted frames? I remember the contempt in the voice of the San Francisco painter Jess, who described to me this one time his work had been taken up by a *très chic* department store in late 50s San Francisco. Back then, it was a city with very few galleries and so a chance to show your work at a department store was about the best a struggling artist could hope for. Jess spent weeks painting the frames to show off his new series of paintings, and the installation went fine. At the opening, however, Jess saw that his strange frames had been sawed off by some tastemakers concerned that they looked sort of, oh I don't know, *amateur.*

Perhaps this is what I should have started out with, in writing about Tony Greene: how deeply California art has invested in failure and contingency. Greene's pictures appear at first so finished and elegant that you don't see the cracks, but they are everywhere you look, in fact, as in the work of Bruce Conner, Jay De Feo, John Baldessari, Simon Rodia, Noah Purifoy, Henrietta Shore, Judith Scott, Raymond Pettibon, Julie Becker, Frances Stark. All of our great artists had an attitude towards the market that was, to one degree or another, a big fuck you. They would make their artwork out of rags and biscuits if they liked, they would make things so ugly and so temporary they would fall apart when you brought them into the light of day. For me the most significant project Tony Greene undertook was his decoration, with Richard Hawkins, of the nonprofit artist-run space LACE in Los Angeles. Given free rein to paint the building as they liked, the artists played it for all its worth, creating a two story mural called "Chains of Bitter Illusion." The building now belongs in private hands; the melancholy yet triumphant remnants of this project are few, faded, scarred by time and weather, and yet they are unspeakably beautiful and precious.

Tony Greene's return in the last couple years has been puzzling on the one hand and comforting on the other. I remember a Queer Nation protest against Cher of all people, Cher who, in a nadir of her endless career, made a skincare infomercial for Aquasentials. In it she claimed to have so few "molecules" she had named them, as if to say, "Yes, I *know* men with AIDS joke about naming their T-cells *and, to tell you the truth, I just don't care!*" We forgave her for voting for Perot but we hit the streets at this one. We were always protesting something and in this case, it seemed to come out all right; we forgave her eventually because she was Cher and maybe we had misunderstood her gobbledygook in the first place? It happens! I for one have never parsed the question about life after love, nor its relevance to, "I can feel something inside of me say, 'I really don't think that you're strong enough.'" I just know that it's the word "really" that's the selling point of the "Believe" lyric.

Tony Greene showed in San Francisco once while he was alive, at Southern Exposure, a group exhibition with Millie Wilson and Doug Ischar. Curators programmed a few events for the show— this was 1988? 1989? At one of them, I was invited to read, along with fellow San Francisco queer writers Bob Glück and Dorothy Allison. Going through my papers recently, I found my folder of poems read that evening. I've put them all in this book you're reading—"Valentine," "Pickpocket," "Marnie and Monotheism," "Don't Look Inside," all the rest; but I close with something new, a poem I wrote in memory of Tony Greene, just a little while ago. Half an hour ago. Forty minutes tops.

Exhausted Autumn

in memory of Tony Greene

While my loans backed up, like sewage, steady my gaze held at a deep
    fixed surface of paint. I watched as invisible strokes poked
    from out of the frame, like tendrils, like the fly—

the green fly of your green jeans,

There was endless and magnificent antiquing in the Valley, Tony,
    —and their tricks are seductive; beware their blue eyes and
    white T-shirts,

cum rags.

They are pollen on the wind of a sky
sky whitened by fog and dawn, ocean miasma,

Surf's up, and the Caravaggio boys ride wave after wave, shorts
    low on their hips,

    Say goodbye, they ain't never looking back

    I spoke their names across a sea of hey, fuck you,

    desperate as a dove,

    and in each frame rolled death, like dice, it rattled like earwigs
on Rod Serling's *Night Gallery,* Laurence Harvey pounding his head
and tearing at his lobes for surcease . . .

    September. October, AIDS came and stalked the land. I had
just about decided fuck school, and then, well,

On the ladder, Tony, halfway up the steps, in jeans,
        are you sleeping?
Today a quaint, pale, alluring reply
        the color of baby aspirin.

In deepest green dusk you marshal your strength,
        September,
Gold lines the backing, as bit by bit you
        lose strength again,
        October,
while whole parts of the body achieve reification,
your lips, Tony, your hands,

those of the man in a Henry Adams
        pilgrimage to Chartres or Mont-Saint-Michel,
the anonymous workers who hammered a scaffold,
and you, on the bottom, holding up your mates, "Wes,"
"Matt," "Ed," and "Joe."

Autumn exhausted, the mute of a deer shy.

Names dissolve into rhymes, "Yes," "That,"
                                        "Dead," "Oh."

Blind faith, head down, and on the wave before you
        a courrèges of white snow, so thin it could be
                white candy

                the skin on Kristeva's cocoa blanc,

What I could see coming was that
I'd be here reading for you still,
today, late at night in San Francisco,

autumn, no leaves, a dark space for white rodents, with eyes like
                crystals in the amazing grave

autumn, bare trees, trunks of birch, round which wobble the cats,
            heehee look drunk, it's like, are they getting picky about
            the forest floor,

The big space that held your works now privatized, a bank of condos,

On the back of your trunks, sagging across your butt like a scaffold,

beautiful name that once spelled the future

THE ELEMENTS

Table of the Elements

It was the elements he got right,
    The strangeness of the new land, its fuzzy things called "trees,"
    the spice in the air, the thick
avocado paste of novelty,
and simultaneously a war to win.
Does it ever leave you, that feeling of having been taken
    hostage by the left, hostage by the right,

sworn to vassalage by your secret tutor, to the undying borders of
    the nation state? Now dry off the elements of tin, mercury, iron,
    oxygen, gold. I was sleeping on a country lawn,
eyes wet with dew, my trousers soaked, my thighs cold,

and a tall animal approacheth, licketh my face clean of soil.

It is the salt of tears for your country, said the wise Platonic antelope.

Down red clay track he raced like a son of a bitch.

*

Like Don Draper, like Anna Madrigal in *Tales of the City*, I dreamed of
  my youth, as an awkward teen raised up in a brothel,

my brother dead, the women I loved lying to me, their silk dresses,

their pale, pink, storebought slips,—but the elements they got right, in
  my dreams they slept and tossed, as up to the star-torn skies we were
  winning a war against dads,

I played piano in the parlor to entertain my dad, as he cracked his
  knuckles against his muscles.

Did this happen, I cried, when I awoke? Or was it but the historical
  materiality of the Cold War that impressed me like Play-Doh,

I'm sorry, Kevin, my father said, you mean Plato, do you not, the name of the Sal Mineo character in *Rebel Without a Cause*, who lied to you,

who wanted James Dean and Natalie Wood as his parents, the philosopher king with the shadows on the cave? Fuck no I mean Play-Doh, dad,

that yellow gooey clay with salty scent that coats one's nostrils like living, that just peels off, that you can put on newspaper and it mirrors the news,

crying the salt of tears for my country,

you could throw it and it would stick to the wall like when pasta is done, said my dad, as in dreams the dead come and animate your bones once again

Down raced the wise antelope, down the red track. "Brother deer," I cried, only to be told that the antelope is not a deer, nor is she my brother. Down she raced like a mad thing, lips afroth with delight.

I stood beside myself in my representation: there were two of me, like Plato's concept of me and my shadow, and someday I'll be a perfected version of that sorry-ass thing I see in the mirror,

speculating and gesticulating with bony fingers and my adam's apple, swallowing up and down, the sign of the liar in panic, in the Platonic mix of flour, water, boric acid, mineral oil, and salt,

my birthright, my dreamright, my clay, yellow clay.

Hydrogen

Seventy five per cent of everything is hydrogen.
Seems like a weighty responsibility for a

colorless gas, but then I think of how wealth
is distributed around the world and how

millions of people slave and don't even have TV,
while a handful of plutocrats grow rich on their labor.

Hydrogen, a low rent element, still gets
to be number one in the famous table

like Christ dominating the Last Supper.
Even *The Da Vinci Code* acknowledges,

that hydrogen is like Jesus, a human god,
one of the people, with the ordinary love impulses

all of us feel. In His case they were for
Judas, the man in the corner, scowling from guilt.

The point is, everyone has those feelings. It's not just
you and me, wandering through this world like

we're invisible, we're neglected, our seminar tanked
and nobody wants to publish our poems.

Tin

Now that's one old fashioned metal I

have to tell you! Do they even
    call tin cans tin cans
    today? In Warhol's day

soup came in tin cans, wrapped
    in paper like a present:

empty, beggars rattled
    change or pencils in them,

monstrously rattling their
    cans, yelling for help.

Tin Man, Rin Tin Tin,
    I'd like to play
    devil's advocate

to argue that tin is
    a thoroughly modern
    element,

But I ain't got nothing.

Emerald

Not an element, according to the internet

but one of the jewels I knew as a little boy,

kids like to know these things, that there's a blue jewel,

I know Mommy—sapphire—and a red jewel—

Ruby—some of these were the names of girls,

There was Pearl Bailey; Topaz, in *I Capture the Castle*,

the artist's model, the earth mother, walking the moors naked

swallowing fog in her teeth, Topaz,

and Emerald Cunard, that's the green jewel, and on

the covers of jazz LPs from the 50s emeralds winked everywhere

it was the color of the magic city that Dorothy and Toto saw,

something fierce about that city, the Wizard was scary,

And where I came from they called the Emerald Isle, as though "Isle" weren't already ridiculous

We lived on Long Island, not even the Irish among us called it "Long Isle."

Maybe that would have made a difference as I grew,

And the mists swirled round my face on the Isle,

I got used to saying "I'll," a homonym,

Oh, I'll suck your cock, Dr. Temple, oh, I'll ace that exam,

Why even study, I'll take that LSD three hundred times that year,

Around me the waves grew in pitch,

Soon it was just me and the emeralds in my pocket,

I came to America and threw them on the ground like Johnny Appleseed,

And from my progress to California came a race of strong robots,

Androids with green eyes, the color of Kermit, but vicious.

I'll never forget them, they make me want to blow.

Shoes, tap three times, bring me back to the place

Where you and you and you were there—and Toto, too.

Gold

Gold, I'm cheating with this since I'm committed to writing on the elements,

Gold, when I was a boy I sought a father figure to paint my body gold, like Shirley Eaton in *Goldfinger*, the spray or stroke that seals off the oxygen, so the girl dies . . .

"You mean like the Oscar," one boy said. "You want to go as the Oscar?"

It was Halloween, night over Smithtown, families stumbling in the dark, skeletons knocking on the doors, an air of excitement over death games,

Games of candy, dropping candy in the pumpkin

"Yes, like the Oscar," I hissed. I wrote about this in first novel, *Shy*.

I never died, I lived through life and its attendant tin fingers,

Olympic gold, or foil, I grew old like a cigarette, chasing the image, went to San Francisco, came to Boulder, at Denver Airport hideous demons and red-eyed horses and gargoyles pluck at your baggage

And I look at them, from the other side of Satan's mask. "Look, could you just do me already? Let's just cut to the chase: press your finger down on spray button, tag me."

Oxygen

Sandra Bullock floating and her colleague (George Clooney) taps her glass

A panic that can still confound her—she had a little daughter died of too much cough syrup in her

oxygen . . . It is the element we throb into life in the union

of sperm and egg

That day I started to breathe through the womb—a gasp blinking through the trailways like a C-section.

Tap, tap, hey are you ready for the gaps in the world? Are you ready to make water, for light, for the twilight? If you slump when it hits your chest, a tower deep will unsheathe you—

enshadow you—Was it only a bird—those wings a-flap?

Oxygen stands for O, for order, for Oprah, she named a whole crumby network after the element—

Stands for orgasm, that little face you wear—that little pout with the tongue tip wet like the—

like the back of a stencil

I could never write a poem, let alone a book, like Perec did with his *A Void*, but banning the "o," Dodie, for then I couldn't put you in it. Or my drone in it, or Mexico, or oxygen. I'd be nowhere and couldn't even say where I was.

For me it would find its life in the

elements

riddles, not jokes; fishes, not loaves;

inside, not out

Sentences, not words; pastures, not woods

Blue, not yellow; midnight, not noon.

Carbon

The dark gray element they make #2 pencils with,

When you stick it in your mouth you could die of carbon poisoning.

The things I believed as a kid, and sometimes, when I least expect it, that kid returns.

They had a cigarette called Lark, with charcoal granules piled into its filter,

and Terry's mother—Mrs. Black—smoked them. Tiny things,

two boys broke twenty cigarettes and collected these specimens of element carbon, sitting wrapped in white paper like a dumpling,

and made a sort of Rembrandt smudge picture of Mrs. Black's dog

on the back of a brown paper bag from the grocery store.

But was that carbon? Terry said, that they use it in carbonated water like ginger ale, but the invisible carbon,

And most carbon's invisible.

It is like racism, you don't notice it until it gets in your hair.

Lithium

He's not making any sense, knowing glance, it's the
lithium. My aunt was like that, you couldn't let her wander the canals, she'd jump in, and look at him,
a complete Syd Barrett. By this time he had pulled down his pants and poured soapy solution down his butt crack and was trying to fart out bubbles, through a little hoop,
I asked him and he said CAConrad recommended this somatic poetry exercise to help heal the straight world.
His little thing was dangling and from behind him rose bubble after bubble, iridescent in the morning sky,
The mountains rose and fell, great slabs of time, like torn tickets heaped by the centuries,
And the sun crawled over my poetry books,
it was pretty like what was the name of that,
it was like yellow bubblicious,
I don't
        think you're ready for this jelly
Cause my body too bootylicious for ya, baby.

Iron

Used to dream of having, not a boyfriend, nor a wife, but an

iron, I would wake up and eat breakfast with. Kitchen iron you could

tilt back (as if on haunches). It would sit on the table, its shiny underside smiling back

at me, we'd talk about what the day would bring, while I ate

eggs and bacon that it, the iron, had prepared before I awoke.

"Breakfast with an Iron."

My friend would turn itself off before I approached so as never to burn me.

Relationships always scared yours truly, the devil in a stewpan,

but with an iron, I felt ironic, in the best sense of the word—

Not the Alanis Morissette track—it was the action of the iron that made it *what I would call "ironic,"*

And not, OMG how ironic, it was the essential core of the iron that

smiled at me, reflected my own teenage face back at me,

but cool and steely in a way I could never be.

I saw *Iron Man 1*, *2*, and *3*, and Iron Man in other shows too, more often than not ironic in the traditional glib way,

Like in *Avengers 2: Age of Ultron*, he gets the idea through unrestrained capitalism to turn on the other avengers,

Even Gwyneth Paltrow, no stranger to *les morts congelés*, or indeed to capital, kind of looks at him, wrinkles her nose,"Tony dear, you have gone too far,"

I have come to your face, the roundabout way,

You I can see reflected in the base of the cool iron, a shiny surface down which the liquid Ultron drips like tears.

They made such a cute couple, when they break up, a little part of me dies.

Wait, is Ultron an element? Do they even *know* at Marvel there's an atomic table?

> —I bet they do.—I'll bet you the whole year I was seventeen that they do know.
>
> I will throw in my Alanis tapes of *Jagged Little Pill*.
>
> I won't need them any more in the new dispensation when I'm married. Maybe it all happened in that one year when I was seventeen and with that year lost, there's a big break in my memories—
>
> The little piece of me that died when you broke up?—slinks towards the borders of an entire year and pushes at them, and eventually, there went detail,

but hello blue sky.

Copper

Copper can't rust and even my abstract dad, my genesis, must have
known that much—Stopping on the way home from my psychiatrist

I bought a pad of paper and two Sharpies, in Mexico.

For Oppen viewed household as hideaway, the inconvenient image
co-terminous with his exile.

How to prevent rust in copper? "In the destructive element immerse."

Conrad wrote that—the Polish one, not the somatic one.

Helium

I have a high voice maybe there's something wrong with my balls and
maybe that's why I'm so shallow

On the other hand I always figured it had something to do with this
bump on the back of my head—sometimes I think my head is so big
because it's so stuffed with the doings of the stars

Or maybe because of Irish tenor blood soaking in my veins

When children poke at me pull on their mother's arm say "Mommy,
Mommy, I'm frightened that man looks like a pig and talks like a
girl," I often say,

"Child you sound more like me than I sound like a girl—and ditto for
your mother, and what pig?"

Ever hear yourself on a tape played back? Well when this happens to me
I hear a chorus of crickets singing

"Take back your mink, take back your pearls"

crickets cacophonous

crickets, false with unbearable affectation,

crisp, arch, keen, clipped halfway between the earth and sky

I hear helium-drunk crickets—insects with rubbing wings running on
that endless Möbius ribbon of time—

I have a voice high as the clouds and a nature low as the slimy trail of
the snail

That's all I have
to cover six feet of self.

Beware the helium trail that spells out your fate in the cloud
like wisps of TV puff

You have it when you're small, like a harelip,

Then you have it when you're a big Alsatian

It is what Hindu legend calls the long body.

The balloon that once blown up assumes a shape and an ending. Pop,
then, deflates your sentence
into mere life.

Tungsten

I had a little workshop in spring,

In a room lined with university press books.

I kept seeing this one book, *Something in the Air*, “something” like *Music*, or *Murder.* I’ll have one more chance to find out since this is my last stop.

The little click in my head, like tungsten, the electric light bulb element, which they stopped making, to rid the planet of rare earth slaves,

deprived of that tungsten click I was no longer sharp.

My beloved students gathered near me, I couldn’t seem to divide them into the hours, and always someone was left out because I babbled too much, and believed there was always one less in the room than there was.

That phantom figure was my mother I think.

She was watching me in Berkeley in springtime, looking over me,

and making sure I did not harm my students with my filaments,

while I told them of my life,

while I told them of the chapbooks of my dreams.

One girl quit; her doing so deflated me, like when you suck all the juice from a mango . . . Peter would not explain or comment, the kinder thing I’m sure, when what you have to say is so bitter. My mother whispers to me in the darkness that that girl did not hate me. She only despised me.

In the curtains of middle age that makes no difference,

But I don't want to tell my mother so, she would feel hurt, ignored.

I want her to be happy, doing the thing she does of guarding me.

She is the alpha and the omega . . . whatever comes beyond Z is her purlieu.

Titanium

This was the track that was playing when the shots began,

at Pulse, in Orlando, the night 49 queers died, "Titanium," by David Guetta,

the ultra-serious David Guetta, from France, with Sia, from Adelaide,

and her words so apropos, or more than she might have thought in 2011, when she wrote those lyrics,

as a metaphor for loving a sociopath I thought, someone "bulletproof," someone made of "titanium,"

the takeaway, for Sia and Guetta, is that you can shoot us but we will never fall.

In the club the dancers heard the shots but some assumed they were part of the mix at Pulse, sound effects for "Titanium,"

there was so much love you could not imagine hate,

the ground was quaking, people waiting outside for their friends or dates or uber cars,

Sia broke down in Denver singing "Titanium" which she dedicated to the 49 slain and the fifty-three injured in Orlando,

you can hear it in her voice, maybe a fear, or guilt, had she written something dumb that came into being,

had she told the world her little secret, and the world, being what it is, had turned on her to prove her wrong?

Sticks and stones may break my bones,
I'm talking loud but ain't saying much.

Like, did you see the video for "Titanium"? A little boy, like ten, the boy from *Super 8*, wakes out of a spell and he's killed every one of the kids in the school, his classmates, and you see the teachers whispering to the cops, they are going to grab this kid and he runs,

Our sympathies are totally with this boy because he didn't even know what his super power was,

Ricochet, you take your aim.

I'll wait for you at Titanium

Through the thin ozone layer that drifts over Orlando stars beam a liquid violet-esque light, like Prince,

as if Prince had been slain. I thought I saw him gasping and gaping,

one hand pressed across Morris Day's mouth, as though to silence him, not because he didn't appreciate his droll chatter,

but that the killer might hear poor Morris babbling,

as though wedged atop the toilet tank as they were, he wanted no sound to issue from under the gray partition and, so, wounded,

in a pool of purple rain and piss,

they both of them died, but saved one man.

That nice young preacher, Brother Taylor, dropped by today

Said he'd be pleased to have dinner on Sunday, oh by the way, where did I put all my plates of titanium, shaped like surfboards, or long cigars

Oh, by the way,

He said he saw a boy looked a lot like you up on Choctaw Ridge,

He said my plates of titanium floated on the muddy waters,

There was so much love you could not imagine hate,

The skies were ripped open,

The clouds eating themselves like the sharks of heaven,

And he and Billie Joe were dropping something off the Tallahatchie Bridge.

Palladium

When I studied the classics with Jason Mitchell, he told me the story of Troy.

Jason was quite a bit younger than I, he had really long hair for a boy called Frank Mills

Troy thought they'd never suffer defeat, for they possessed the wooden amulet

bestowed on them by Pallas Athene, as if to say, you Troy, are my favorite city.

Jason told me of a shower curtain in Brooklyn, on which the names and number of the elements were laid bare.

Odysseus, he said, and Diomedes who slew the bull, went into Troy and took the wooden Palladium.

I picture it as my lucky charm, the thing that has kept me from ruin,

Made out of wood, like the imaginary fence made of sticks left over from all the Good Humor bars I ate as a lad of Jason's age.

Without my shield the wind and the rain, and AIDS, would surely have gotten me. It was kind of a delusional Troylike feeling,

to think that shield would always be there.

Two Greeks stole it from me, I'm like that girl in *Hair* who sings,

"I would gratefully appreciate it if you see them tell them that Jason and I are in the park, we don't want our two dollars back, just our

wood protection." It was like the old days, when Judy was alive,

—Judy Garland: when she needed to make a comeback, she'd always

wake and ask for the Palladium.

Silver

"When I think of Bill Berkson I think of his smile, and when I think of his smile I think of white clouds, drifting by the Chrysler Building . . .

There was something of the Chrysler Building in Bill; they shared the element of silver."

—Nathaniel Dorsky, at Bill's memorial,
San Francisco Art Institute, July 24, 2016

Lead

Latin word "Plumbum" translates to "liquid silver," so hello Plumbum, PB they call you on the table—the periodic table.

We book people think of "pb" as paperback when deciding whether to spring for a hardcover book, or should I go for the pb.

And we who have kids think of pb as peanut butter, for it's always time to put some pb&j on the table,—not the periodic table.

But lead, I don't know, one morning I woke and opened the door on my landing, in the distance two towers and the moon rising, the supermoon the biggest since 1948, and bells rang of lead,

Elderly magazine sang of lead,

I emptied the whole shebang of lead,

rung down like a metal door by the Trump campaign, the surprising election of Trump,

—as, in the middle of the sixties, my dad stood by silently on the outside of the track while I ran the 100 yard dash.

I didn't come in last exactly, but my little short legs never get me anywhere.

He wouldn't embarrass me in public, but on the way home in the VW he said, "They call it a 'dash' for a reason."

I sulked, staring out the side window at a heap of Long Island trees and branches and flowers and squirrels, driveways, gravestones, lawns and woods, ever changing.

Like frames of film in a Super 8,

He says, "C'mon, Kev, get the lead out of your ass just one time."

When did he die? I didn't even remember, but he was better off, for I made him angry with my ways. I was so aimless, I would never be an engineer.

I didn't even know the word but it was flâneur.

Above us the supermoon beat down, bigger than any moon since 1948, and that was when he was alive but I was not yet born.

They were the changes in the world, an hour of gold mutating to an hour of lead, like alchemy in reverse, how you play with the devil's bargain.

I was the chicken who failed to cross the road, just stood there, dumb and feckless, the lead in my ass virulent, aesthetic, a throb, a stance, total Bartleby, a reactor.

About a year later I was hitching back to Smithtown when a Volkswagen bug slowed down, the window dropped, a pair of sunglasses looked out at me, came to a halt.

This turned out to be Justin, from Switzerland, who became my first Swiss boyfriend. Slowly in the car he told me that in Switzerland they didn't grow boys like me, I was this American family, genus and species, superb example like a butterfly. Next to the old graveyard, on Landing Avenue, I blushed in hot twilight. I was shy but not very, it wasn't even half an hour when he asked me what my ass looked like.

Seemed so strange we were in a VW bug, the same model my dad drove. I shucked off my pants, dragged my underwear down to my knees, and sat on Justin's Swiss hand. Like a Swiss watch, baby.

Afterwards a confidant told me it was unlikely that Justin was really Swiss, as it is a name totally unknown in the land of the Alps and the skis and the liars. No matter, he was taller than I and twice my age and I was totally his American butterfly boy, in the tenth grade and my ass, he swore, was the most beautiful he had ever seen even in Europe.

Here comes the distortion of Cronos, as payback descends, and the cruel among us rise from their slime and take their places on the ceiling, to slop down on our faces.

Here comes the night, a blindfold tied round our heads and knotted

behind the ears.

Turn over the card, it's the hanged man, it's Villon:

My name's François, which is ludicrous,

Born in Paris, near Pontoise,

And from this six foot length of rope,

My neck will find out how much my ass weighs.

Mercury

When I broke the glass of thermometer, out ran the mercury,

In one liquid blob, matter calling to matter, like not one of its molecules wanted to be parted from another even for a moment.

Mercury was supposed to be so mercurial—like Ariana Reines, the poet who,

we were celebrating her book *Mercury*, in Chicago for the AWP,

She and Dodie and Peter, and Lewis Warsh, reading together in a bar and she cancelled, due to snow in New York, but the crowd learned that she had deputized Thurston Moore to read for her,

So they were assuaged, but then it turned out Thurston

had missed the same plane. Joel Craig the emcee came out and had to announce that they wouldn't be getting Ariana, *nor Thurston*,

but me, and this one woman, sitting at a round table by herself next to the mic, by herself except fourteen bottles of beer surrounded her, when

she heard the news she smashed a bottle on the table and screamed, "Fuck that," and bolted into the snow, so I got up and read thinking, worst auspices ever . . .

My mind ran clear and I declared to myself I would be Ariana for half an hour,

just assume her identity. To my aid came Thespis on silvery wings, I was more Ariana than she herself had ever been I'm sure, and as I spoke her words I understood the difficult section of Mercury called "Thursday" as has nobody else before or since. I was writing it on stage, live, giving it to my fans, word by word, and I realized that he, the missing Thurston, was the god they had coined the word "Thursday" after,

for he would bless us on a Thursday if we leaned on him

it could be any day of the week,

it could be all the molecules in his body entering and filling mine,

I would be a day. I'd run around after myself. I would cohere.

When I finished, the silence swelled around me, profound, then a burst of sustained applause, and even the woman out in the snow was sobbing, for she hadn't heard me.

Calcium

for Veronica De Jesus

Roy Halladay died today and I think of you, Veronica De Jesus, how you knew he was basically the coolest white man to ever walk the earth,

Today his biplane Icon A5 flipped, crunched and crashed into six feet of water (how did they even know it was him? Perhaps from his golden red hair, like a dog's,

and his perfect white teeth, like a cat's, a ginger cat, calcium

thick on 'em like barnacles, white barnacles, ivory. He smelled like milk and gold, like those chocolate half dollars wrapped in gold foil).

At the press conference, the sheriff winced at the mike, and unexpectedly, he revealed he had known the dead pitcher, known him in Pasco County,

and he was the most decent man in sports and in Florida. We was just fishing for charity Sunday.

I know all them people are in each other's pockets, you don't take home the Cy Young trophy twice without being in bed with the sheriff's department,

And still I thought of you, Veronica, and how on Facebook, the Philadelphia poet Pattie McCarthy remembered,

"I think his perfect game was on the night of a Chapterhouse reading. Kevin went to the reading & I stayed home with the babies (only one baby maybe?). He walked in the door at the last out & I was weeping. I actually cried."

Kevin Varrone wrote, "Not Doc—say it ain't so. Just want to drink a beer and watch him pitch all night—not when he was perfect, but when he wasn't, when he struggled, when he was human—which for me was when he was most perfect."

You have the knack of making them seem alive again, the dead ones, the ones you draw in memoriam:

> I remember your Larry Sultan, in a windbreaker on a beach pier, just a suggestion of face, the walk was enough
>
> And Tura Satana from *Faster, Pussycat! Kill! Kill!*, all struggle and snapping a dude's wrist off if he gave her any shit.
>
> And Ruth Asawa sewing herself a tiny basket and a pneumatically bobbing gas balloon to travel out far over our heads—up to the aether—

Or Donna Summer, and Etta James, at Margaret Tedesco's space—a feeling for disco, a feeling for tortured soul. "Last Dance," in purple, green and gray.

Over grinning of a rictus face—calcium.

Carnivalesque march of Bakhtin through a zoo—black bars, white snow.

Calcium light pouring from a drainpipe, onto a tintype, as images melt in white watery streaks, like the sweat of the gods.

I couldn't see the ball where Doc threw it into the future. Where, in that impossible galley, I've absolutely lost it.

Let the Biblical veil of Veronica tell his perfect game, let those moved by legend and myth come forward to seal it away, like seaweed in stone, calcium, bone.

Cobalt

I met him on the bus, beg pardon you said, but don't you know Karla
Milosevich? We've met before—on this bus, the 27

We were standing, hanging on to straps, two guys of Irish ancestry, you,
David

Your quiet voice like some John Ford film of early 50s,

Quiet, but inside great depths like the craters of the moon.

How is it that one bus from 5th and Folsom, down to that block that
Truck (the gay bar) was on, the great "Truc-kay," it takes maybe 10
minutes, but in two different worlds. In one, Japanese auto stencillers
melt endless strips of UV ribbon to the windows of pimp rides?

On the other, stately David Cunningham Projects, I saw the weirdest
fucking objects in the world, my eyes went up in fumes like clay,

And your quiet exegeses like this was all reasonable and Kenneth
Anger the Ken Burns of documentary vision.

Three gold figures, slight, like hairs in a locket. Three gold figures, the
initials of your monogram, DCP

In Melbourne, in a studio space

At night the boys want the same thing, the girls know how to please
them,

And I'll do it, but I've got to be certain,

My hair is frizzing up like a poodle, maybe in Australia the curl is
racially inflected, like a wave, like the name, "Kylie," said to mean
"boomerang" in Maori, then what language is "boomerang" in?

In what language is the cliché of having been burnt before

by heartless boys with vexed cocks a thing? Can you make it come alive by feeling it on video, to a jigsaw beat? Down Melbourne Keys she runs in heels,

fairly desperate like Joan Fontaine in *Letter from an Unknown Woman*, but in teals and salmons and crushed roses nailed to the side of her head, eyes cobalt, the darker of two midnight blues.

She is still learning how to enslave the camera guy, the Paul Levack of her little world.

In a minute she will touch his top.

Cobalt II

Erik Killmonger, go master the element given to a hungry nation by meteor shower,

right—they called it vibranium? It muffles sound and even better,

it refigures and realigns with itself to become ever stronger, like titanium.

Can outside nations buy vibranium, or is it just there to protect the fog-shrouded people of Wakanda?

Justice warrior Killmonger is all like, break the fog, unleash

oceans of vibranium to give black folk world over a decent chance at life.

Superpowers for all, not just T'Challa—Black Panther—and the coterie of his family and kin.

Here in the real world, we have cobalt in the Congo,

unfortunately mined by child slaves,

and coveted by white techno superman Elon Musk who wants to use it past our iPhones, he has promised Earth the "Tesla."

Sad little car,

o what a mess this whole energy business is,

perhaps covert funding of rebel groups in the Congo will divert cobalt from the berserk dictator who runs the country, into the hands of white energy savants like Musk.

He can only control the cobalt supplies of two nations, ours and theirs.

I don’t know what’s right, Erik Killmonger.

Elon Musk, you are the white anti-metal man found in Antarctica under sheets of old ice, like Isak Dinesen.

Arsenic

The boy and girl have been having sex for a

long time: an hour? Forty minutes?

Practiced roués, but somehow caught past understanding;

out of their league, unable to come. It's like their limbs

plug up with arsenic. "Are you OK?" I say.

"This is enough okay for now," Dodie replies.

Fluorine

Is fluoride a compound?

Since I've committed to writing a serial poem about the elements,

Hell must freeze over before I stoop to writing about mere compounds,
much as they are precious to me, dearer to my heart some of them
than some of the so called "elements."

Every time you see a yellow gas, it's fluorine,

Rocking the letter "f" and the low, low chemical number 9.

Zirconium

for Anselm Berrigan

Just when you think something is real,
stable,
a diamond

it turns out to be cubic . . .
cubic
zirconium. When does our luck

change, Anselm? Is that
willow tree still weeping
there? Two lifetimes I've

spent hunting the fake and
pasting glitter into the
holes. Does that laddie

with the twinkling eye
sad and happy not
to see me there.

Next time our luck will
change: I'll knock on the rock,
a huge crevice will appear,

with you in it, like that old-
time sword standing up.
The past and present king,

once and future Spring.

Silicon

Sara, I love ice creeping over napalm, an acrostic that begins with your
name, and continues with six more words, the initial letters

of which,

spell out "silicon" just like the native valley where we live and learn
from.

Silicon valley, like nothing on earth, revolves around a few famous
legends, compare it to the poetry world with Claudia Rankine to the
East and Ferlinghetti to the west, from M. NourbeSe Philip in the
North to, who's a southern poet, oh, Sandra Simonds.

However it profits from the genius of Christian Bök who invented the
whole shebang once upon a time, in a garage band with Steve Jobs
and Bill Gates and Woz,

a boys club, Sara, from which the figures of Ada Lovelace and those
women of Cape Canaveral have been hidden, occluded.

Scenting their little boxes in their garages in that valley,

we began to live like the little foxes of the Bible, first chasing our tails,
then chasing

the rare earth elements that nothing human should possess. Leave sili-
con to the

hidden spirits of the earth that brought its scent to linger among us,

let the nature of information gathering systems eat themselves up,

and how is this like poetry? Every day we think about Studio One and
try to come up with better answers for our children, and we look at
the few remaining animals of world, and weep,

strange tears of silicon like Man Ray pebbles on our faces. Sara, I look
inside crude occlusions now.

SELECTED BIBLIOGRAPHY

POETRY

Les éléments. France: Editions Joco Seria, 2017.
Tony Greene Era. Wonder Books, 2017.
Tweaky Village. Wonder Books, 2014.
Action Kylie. In Girum Imus Nocte et Consumimur Igni, 2008.
Argento Series. Krupskaya Press, 2001.

PROSE

Selected Amazon Reviews. Semiotext(e), 2024.
Fascination: Memoirs. Semiotext(e), 2018.
Spreadeagle. Publication Studio, 2012.
Impossible Princess. City Lights Books, 2009.
I Cry Like a Baby. Painted Leaf Press, 2001.
Poet Be Like God: Jack Spicer and the San Francisco Renaissance (with Lewis Ellingham). Wesleyan University Press, 1998.
Arctic Summer. Hard Candy, 1997.
Little Men. Hard Press, 1996.
Santa. Leave Books, 1995.
Bedrooms Have Windows. Amethyst Press, 1989.
Shy. Crossing Press, 1989.
Desirée. e.g. Press, 1986.

PLAYS

Stage Fright: Selected Plays from San Francisco Poets Theater. Kenning Editions, 2019.

Island of Lost Souls. Nomados, 2003.
Often (with Barbara Guest). Kenning Editions, 2001.
Stone Marmalade (with Leslie Scalapino). Singing Horse Press, 1996.

AS EDITOR

Writers Who Love Too Much: New Narrative Writing 1977-1997 (co-edited with Dodie Bellamy). Nightboat Books, 2017.
The Kenning Anthology of American Poets Theater 1945-1985 (co-edited with David Brazil). Kenning Editions, 2010.
My Vocabulary Did This to Me: The Collected Poetry of Jack Spicer (co-edited with Peter Gizzi). Wesleyan University Press, 2008.
Sam D'Allesandro, The Wild Creatures. Suspect Thoughts Press, 2005.

Born on Christmas Eve, **KEVIN KILLIAN** (1952–2019) grew up on Long Island before moving to San Francisco in 1980, where he abandoned his doctoral dissertation to become a poet. In the Bay Area literary scene of the time his writing stood out immediately for its strangeness and humor, its frankness and mutability. The largely queer ferment from which that work emerged came to be known as New Narrative. With his wife, Dodie Bellamy, he coedited *Writers Who Love Too Much: New Narrative 1977–1997*. In addition to publishing poetry, short stories, and novels, Kevin also wrote and produced fifty plays and was a preeminent scholar on the poet Jack Spicer. He published hundreds of issues of his legendary literary magazine *Mirage Periodical* (using the Xerox machine at his day job); curated art shows; ran a number of reading series; and mentored countless younger poets, writers, and artists. He took hundreds of nude photographs of writers and artists, later collected as *Tagged*, and wrote over two thousand Amazon customer reviews, posthumously published as *Selected Amazon Reviews*. Kevin also published criticism in *Art in America*, *Artforum*, *Art Week*, *The Brooklyn Rail*, *BOMB*, and elsewhere. His memorial service was held at the San Francisco Museum of Modern Art.

EVAN KENNEDY is a poet and bicyclist living in San Francisco. Most recently, he is the author of *Metamorphoses* (2023).

JASON MORRIS is the author of ten books and chapbooks, including *Attending Void* (2025), *Low Life* (2021), and *Levon Helm* (2018). He lives in San Francisco.

KAY GABRIEL is a writer and organizer. She's the author of *Perverts* (2025), *Kissing Other People or the House of Fame* (2023), and *A Queen in Bucks County* (2022), all from Nightboat. She's the Editorial Director at the Poetry Project and lives in New York City.

NIGHTBOAT BOOKS

Nightboat Books, a nonprofit organization, seeks to develop audiences for writers whose work resists convention and transcends boundaries. We publish books rich with poignancy, intelligence, and risk. Please visit nightboat.org to learn about our titles and how you can support our future publications.

The following individuals have supported the publication of this book. We thank them for their generosity and commitment to the mission of Nightboat Books:

George Albon, Kazim Ali, Ava Aviva Avnisan, Jean C. Ballantyne, Rumeli Banik, Julia Bloch, Will Blythe, Kris Brandenburger, David Buuck, Rob Byrnes, Philip Clark, V. Shannon Clyne, Theodore Cornwell, Drew Cushing & Ralph Burr, Bruno Franco, Gisela Gamper, Susan Gevirtz, Photios Giovanis, Peter Gizzi, Matt Gordon, Amanda Greenberger, Garth Greenwell, David Groff, Jonathan Groff, Rob Halpern & Lee Azus, Daniel Handler, Sarah Heller, Colin Herd, Karen Holtzman, Colter Jacobsen & Lawrence Rinder, Parag Rajendra Khandhar, Sue Landers, Katy Lederer, Shari Leinwand, Daniel Levine, Elizabeth Madans, Ricardo Maldonado, Douglas A. Martin, Pooja Mehta, Ethan Mitchell, Carol Mirakove, Caren Motika, Elizabeth Motika, Asker Saeed, Michael Sasso, The Leslie Scalapino - O Books Fund, Amy Scholder, Adie Steckel, Eric Suchyta, Conrad Tao, Benjamin Taylor, Mohan Trivedi, Divya Victor, Jerrie Whitfield & Richard Motika, Patrick Whitgrove, Jacob Wick, Clay Williams

This book is made possible, in part, by grants from the New York City Department of Cultural Affairs in partnership with the City Council, the New York State Council on the Arts Literature Program, and the Topanga Fund, which is dedicated to promoting the arts and literature of California.